Merry
Christmas,
1999

Create Your
Personal
Sacred Text

Love,

BROADWAY BOOKS
NEW YORK

Create Your Personal Sacred Text

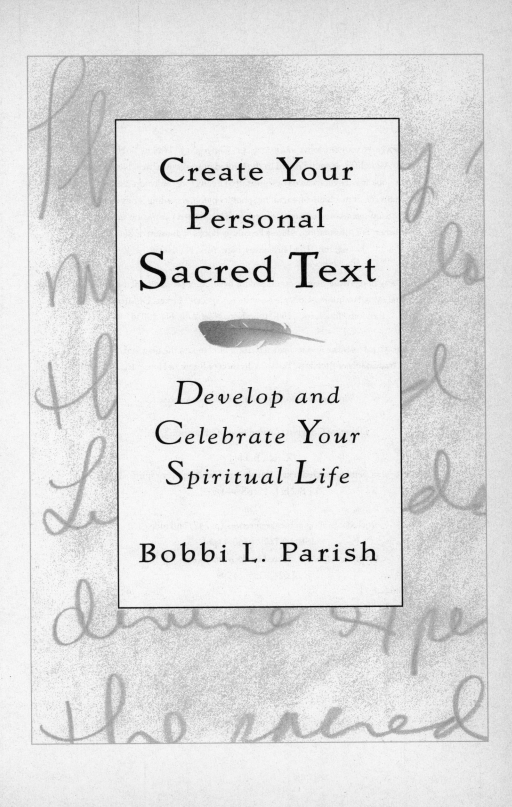

Develop and Celebrate Your Spiritual Life

Bobbi L. Parish

BROADWAY

Broadway Books titles may be purchased for business or promotional use or for special sales. For information, please write to: Special Markets Department, Random House, Inc., 1540 Broadway, New York, NY 10036.

BROADWAY BOOKS and its logo, a letter B bisected on the diagonal, are trademarks of Broadway Books, a division of Random House, Inc.

Visit our website at www.broadwaybooks.com

Library of Congress Cataloging-in-Publication Data

Parish, Bobbi L.
Create your personal sacred text : develop and celebrate your spiritual life / by Bobbi L. Parish. —1st ed.
p.   cm.
Includes bibliographical references (p. 247) and index.
ISBN 0-7679-0368-4 (pb)
1. Spiritual life.   2. Sacred books Miscellanea.   I. Title.
BL624.P335   1999
291.4′46—dc21   99-24026
                                                                                        CIP

FIRST EDITION

Book design by DEBORAH KERNER

99 00 01 02 03   10 9 8 7 6 5 4 3 2 1

To Gabrielle,
who always
had faith in my journey

Contents

Preface

ON A WARM SUMMER evening six years ago I sat in my living room, keeping company with a quart of gin and 250 assorted pills. Over the last several years I had witnessed my once-charmed life crumble while I descended into hell. For two and a half decades I tried to squeeze myself into the mold of perfection, believing the message of my family's god that nothing less was acceptable. I grew up striving to meet that unattainable goal, thinking that if I could just manage to become flawless I would finally win the love of my family, my friends, and my god. I went to the right schools, got the best grades, earned two degrees in four years, married an upwardly mobile man, and established myself in a lucrative career.

As bright and shiny as I appeared on the outside, inside was a creative and vibrant woman slowly suffocating under the expectations and ideals of others. Every once in a while she would raise her head and ask, "Now? Am I okay now? Do you love me now?" Over time the questions came less frequently, and eventually, too weary to even lift her head, she stopped asking them altogether.

The constant mental and emotional gymnastics did not earn me any substantive approval or love. Instead, they wore me out. Three years into my marriage I was diagnosed with severe depression. I was utterly humiliated because this was obvious proof that my efforts to attain perfection, and the elusive approval of my god, had failed. My idyllic career began to disintegrate as I struggled to concentrate and juggle multiple tasks. A year later my husband had had enough. I was not turning out to be the witty, charming, and socially engaging lawyer's wife he had envisioned. He left me for a young college coed.

The path of my descent got steeper. I lost my footing and tumbled, careering off rocks and outcroppings as I traveled farther into the depths of depression. As hard as I tried to catch myself and arrest my fall, I could not find a solid hand- or foothold anywhere.

My career finally collapsed—further proof of my failure. Afraid to fire me, the company put me in a variety of make-work positions. As a result of the divorce, my finances reached a desperate point. My humiliation grew deeper. My life was moving farther and farther away from perfection and, consequently, farther and farther away from the love I so ardently desired.

Feeling helpless and desperate, I returned to church and prayed to the god of my family. I confessed every sin I could imagine I had committed and begged for forgiveness. On my knees, and at times prostrate on the floor, I pleaded for mercy. The priests and nuns had always said that the way to god's heart was through self-denial and service to others. I threw myself into activities at the church, searching for the elusive road to perfection.

A ray of hope appeared. A man I knew from work, someone I had always considered a kindred spirit, asked me out on a date. He pursued me with fervor, sending me flowers and telling me he loved me.

It was at once wonderful and frightening. Here was a chance to right all the wrongs and prove to the world that I was not worthless. But it was also another opportunity to falter and see my heart betrayed.

That thought terrified me. I had so little emotional energy left, not enough to weather one more storm. Yet when he proposed marriage I ignored my fear and said yes. Immediately he waffled. "Maybe you're right. Maybe it *is* moving too fast." He had set the trap and I walked right into it. As the steel jaws clamped shut I tumbled backward, no longer bumping along the hill but now free-falling into a bottomless pit.

I returned to church and sought counsel from the minister. He talked to me of the sin of despair as it represented a failure to trust in god. I needed to renew my efforts to help others and put my needs for love aside. I tried a therapy group. The counselors led us in playing musical chairs and countless craft projects. While that helped pass the time, it did not ease my pain. The only thing I learned was how to concoct a lethal mixture of over-the-counter medication from a fellow patient.

My fiancé and I made a date to discuss our relationship and its direction. I drove to his house hopeful that if I pleaded my case well enough, I could still make things okay. But within moments of my arrival he told me he had started seeing someone else, that he could be my friend but nothing more.

My vision doubled. Before me stood not just him but my ex-husband. Both rejecting me. Both betraying me. And behind them, looming the largest and darkest of all, was the god of my family. All were handing down verdicts of worthlessness. The evidence was overwhelming, and I did not possess the energy to cross-examine any more witnesses or present any more arguments. I accepted the judgment from what I believed was a jury of my peers, and without a word in reply turned and left his house to carry out my sentence. This time he did not pursue me.

I stopped at the drugstore on my way home, picking up the combination of medications I had learned about a few days before. In my apartment I dumped them all into a bowl while I recorded a suicide note on my cassette deck. As I swallowed the pills, helped along by mouthfuls of gin, I raged against my lousy life and the god who had betrayed and abandoned me.

My memory of the next hour is fuzzy. Somehow I made it upstairs to my bedroom, determined to die there with the door shut so my cat wouldn't be confronted with my dead body. But like a bolt from the blue I was suddenly filled with panic—afraid to die. My last conscious memory is of calling 9-1-1 and asking for help, unsure whether there was any reason to save me but determined to try to find one if I survived.

When I awoke in intensive care the next morning, I vowed to search out the one thing that I believed I needed to survive: a healthy, vibrant, loving relationship with a Higher Power. I was raised Catholic and spent most of my adult life in conservative, evangelical Protestant denominations. So I felt I would not find the kind of god I sought in my past or current faith. My suicide attempt shook me to the core, catapulting me into several long, hard years of self-examination and reconstruction.

I began asking questions in earnest, seeking the Spirit I believed existed but that I had not yet encountered (or so I thought). Quickly I realized that the god I had been raised to believe in was man-made, a façade of doctrine and dogma so thick that his true nature was barely perceivable. My experiences with him had always been through an intermediary—a priest, a minister, or a teacher.

By the time his messages reached me, they were garbled and contorted by someone else's perception or ego. It was like the game you play as a child where one person whispers a message in someone's ear who whispers it in someone else's ear and so on until it is said aloud by the person at the end, evoking fits of laughter at how mixed up it had become along the way. Somewhere at the beginning of things Jesus had said, "I am the light of the world," but by the time it reached me it sounded something like "Give some pipe to a squirrel."

Raised to be obedient, I tried to comply with these man-made interpretations of divine guidance. I performed the rituals, memorized the prayers, and obeyed the guidelines. Not surprisingly, these activities did not bring me the peace and love I was seeking. Tired of working through intermediaries, I threw out all of my conceptions of Spirit and sought to make direct, face-to-face contact.

I started to read about different spiritual traditions, looking for guidance on my quest. Surely others had made this same journey and recorded their experience. I explored East and West, searching from ancient to contemporary time. As I moved into the study of sacred texts, I was astonished to find amazing commonalties between them. Here was an infinite river of truth—a universal wisdom—that flowed underneath every spiritual tradition.

I began to envision the authors of all sacred texts and the great wisdom teachers as drillers of wells. They had bored through the earth, brought up water, and told others what their experience was like. Their teachings consisted of their perceptions of how the water tasted, how it felt in their bodies, and how it affected them. Because we are all unique creatures, they each had a different encounter with the River of Truth. But the source was constant and unchanging. Unfortunately, I had experienced it only through the well drilled by conservative, legalistic churches, and even then what was shared with me had gone through so many hands that it had lost the integrity of the original message. As a result, I had constructed a very narrow and self-destructive view of Spirit.

Through my exploration I was finally able to see how much of my personal power I had relinquished to those I had been told had all the answers: clergy, teachers, men, and the adults in my family. I had allowed them to define me, my life and values, my view of the world and my relationship with Spirit. They told me that they had the keys to the vaults that contained all the answers to my questions, but I could not have access to them because I was young, imperfect, female, divorced. I was too flawed for God to be available to me.

Yet as I searched I found that not only were there no locks on the vault, but there was not even a door. My gender, my lifestyle, my mistakes, or my marital status did not block my path. As hard as I had been searching for her, Spirit had been seeking me. The answers had never been in someone else's hand. They were right before me and inside me all along.

I began to drink deeply from every well I could find. I read the writings of medieval Christian mystics and Islamic Sufi poets. I examined the poetry and essays written by contemporary spiritual leaders. Over time I dug my own tunnels down to the water, by meditating upon and contemplating what I was reading, making the direct contact with Spirit that I so desired. As I explored the River of Truth from every vantage point and angle, not only did my understanding of Spirit deepen and widen, but also my relationship with him exploded with vibrant energy. My depression lifted.

I started collecting excerpts from songs, books, and sacred texts that reflected the growing body of truth I was discovering. I have a beautiful song from Sinead O'Connor's *Gospel Oak* album entitled "This Is to Mother You." To me it speaks of the maternal nature of Spirit and her desire to protect and nurture. It so powerfully captures my thoughts about those issues that after countless readings it still moves me to tears.

I also have a poem by nineteenth-century writer Ella Wheeler Wilcox, "As If by Fire," that talks about the paradox of suffering and growth. Then there are my own essays and poems about survival and celebration after enduring so much. Some of the selections are several pages, some only a few sentences. I began recording my experiences in a variety of forms: poetry, essays, songs, and prayers. I wrote about the lessons that I learned and the wisdom that I gained as I sought a healthy relationship with Spirit. Adding those to the excerpts of others' material, I soon had a collection of work that reflected my journey to the River of Truth. I used it to focus and develop my growing spiritual life. The concept of a personal sacred text was born.

Acknowledgments

THERE ARE CERTAINLY many people who have contributed to this book's becoming a reality. Not all of them have been a positive influence, but even the bad experiences have impacted this process by providing me with opportunities to grow. I acknowledge all of them—not just those whose names I list. These individuals have contributed so significantly that I can recognize parts of what they have given me in the book. Not to mention them by name would be like not citing an author whose work I quote.

To Meredith Bernstein, my agent, who saw the potential in this project immediately and invested her time and reputation in it.

To Tracy Behar, my editor at Broadway, and her assistant, Angela Casey, who walked me through the book publishing process and helped shape an initial draft of the manuscript into a work I could be proud of.

To the Reverend Bruce Robinson, minister at The Living Enrichment Center, who was the second person I told about my conviction to write this book and who supported me from the outset—if he had not responded positively I might not have had the courage to continue.

To Kim Waters, my sister, who supported and encouraged me through the good times and the bad.

To Tom Waters, my brother-in-law, who is my friend and faithful computer consultant, saving me from more than one technological disaster.

To Tommy Waters, my nephew, who provides me with immeasurable joy and makes me the proudest aunt in the world.

To Jeanne Klahn, my friend, colleague, and fellow seminarian, who supported me even when it was not popular to do so.

To all my clients, who taught me about courage, perseverance, and victory in the face of enormous tragedy and loss; thank you especially to those who allowed me to share their work or story in this book.

To Mary Manin Morrissey, the founder and senior minister at The Living Enrichment Center, who gave me her wisdom, guidance, support, and encouragement before she'd even met me in person.

To Stan Logie, who has provided immeasurable encouragement and support for my journey, helping me realize that despite the past I am both lovable and capable of loving unconditionally. You are my personal angel.

And absolutely most of all, to Gabrielle Franke, my therapist, who gave selflessly of herself for many years so that I had a safe and loving space to build a life worth living. As a therapist myself I know how hard it is to sit with someone in terrible emotional pain, especially if there are no ready, easy answers. The temptation is great to pull away or become clinically detached rather than remain fully present and engaged. But she never flinched. Instead, she stood right beside me, face into the wind, against the fiercest of storms. On several occasions she even put her professional reputation on the line to advocate against some powerful and nasty opponents for my receiving appropriate attention and care. When I couldn't love myself she loved me, when I couldn't manage my life she helped me open my mail and make phone calls, when I couldn't pray she prayed for me, and when I didn't have the will to fight she took my place. I know that through it all she suffered, at times greatly, but she never withdrew and she never gave up on me. And it was that constant unconditional loving that helped me find the courage to embark on my journey to the River of Truth and into the light. I have life because she was willing to be an angel in my life. Few people in this world can point to one person and say "Because of you I live today." Gabrielle is that person for me. This book is as much hers as it is mine and to her I lovingly dedicate it.

Create Your Personal Sacred Text

Introduction

THIS BOOK is my effort to pass on the power of creating a personal sacred text to you, the reader. It maps my journey, and that of my clients, and walks you through the process, step by step, of selecting material from other sources and writing your own scripture. Then it gives you many options for using your text both individually and communally to integrate its message into your daily life.

I have been using the process of creating a personal sacred text personally and professionally, with the clients in my therapy practice, for more than a decade. We have all found it to be transformative. Given the opportunity to develop a text that reflects our unique relationship with Spirit, rather than to try to make one already in existence fit our experience, we found our spiritual practices and beliefs renewed and revitalized. Those who had never had faith in a Higher Power found the process to be a simple and practical way of exploring and developing various spiritual concepts. It was so easy to personalize according to each individual's needs that even my clients who had been devastated by trauma and abuse found creating their own sacred text to be a safe method of redefining their place in the world.

Based on my personal story and the stories of my clients, you may be tempted to think this activity is only for the wounded. It isn't. This is not simply a self-help book in spiritual wrapping. It is a spiritual process that seeks a broader and deeper relationship with Spirit. Through the process, you will experience a variety of benefits, such as increased self-awareness and a greater capacity to relate to loved ones. For me the greatest impact has been the healing of my connection with Spirit. For you it may be different. Having problems and being in therapy are not prerequisites for the journey.

This is not a book about theology or doctrine. I won't attempt to convert you to my beliefs or demand that you read my favorite books. Creating a personal sacred text is just that: personal. It's not about me. It's about you and your journey to the River of Truth, whatever shape or form that takes. We are each unique and valuable. Each of our stories matters in the universe. You deserve to have a sacred text that reflects your uniqueness and tells your story. I will provide you with road maps and a guidebook. But the quest is your own. Start where you are and move in whatever direction you feel led.

Everyone is welcome. You need not have read one sentence of sacred literature or written one line of poetry. I will give you all the tools you will need. If you have explored these areas already, great. There are beginning, intermediate, and advanced resources in every section. Not only is this a personal process, it is also a dynamic one. It will grow and change with you as you make your journey, expanding and contracting as needed.

You also don't need to have huge chunks of time available to create a personal sacred text. In today's hectic world I doubt any one of us has hours to spend reading volumes of poetry in one sitting. That's okay. This journey adapts to the time you do have available. It is not an intellectual or analytical process that can be rushed to completion, given adequate mental focus. Instead, it is a mystical voyage of the heart and soul, which operate on a whole different time line from your brain. A half hour here and an hour there over the course of several weeks or months will do just fine.

Because I have purposely sought to construct a process that welcomes people of all faith traditions, I use spiritual terms and concepts that are as inclusive as possible. For example, there are many names for the Spirit presence we call God, Allah, our Higher Power, or Great Spirit. Some may not believe in a Spirit other but instead refer to the Infinite or their Higher Self. In seeking a referent that would be as inclusive as possible, I settled on Spirit. Out of respect for all genders I will switch back and forth between using masculine and feminine pronouns. For some of you this may be uncomfortable, but it would be a great opportunity to begin expanding your concept of Spirit.

Perhaps you are uneasy exploring the sacred literature of other faiths or are uncomfortable with the concept of writing your own scripture. Many of us grew up being taught that both of these ideas are heretical and/or blasphemous. That's fine. As I said, start where you are and move where you feel led. There are no right or wrong ways to create a personal sacred text, and it may take some time for you to become comfortable with the process of creating your text.

The book is organized to aid in the creation of your personal sacred text. Part One provides all of the preliminary details you would normally seek before deciding to embark on such a project, including definitions and descriptions of the process. Part Two describes how to assemble and format your sacred text. Parts Three and Four show you how to embark on the journey, gather materials from existing sources, and write your own scripture. Part Five describes uses for your sacred text.

Now I would like to invite you into the powerful process of creating a personal sacred text. I know of no better words to use than those of the Reverend Mary Manin Morrissey, senior minister at my spiritual home, The Living Enrichment Center, and author of *Building Your Field of Dreams*: "Whoever you are and wherever you are on your journey of faith, you are welcome here."

PART ONE

~

An Overview
of the
Creation Process

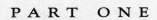

*For me, God and truth
are convertible terms.
Devotion to the truth is
the sole reason for our existence.*

— MOHANDAS K. GANDHI

ONE

Defining the
Personal
Sacred Text

FINALLY. You made it home. After a grueling day at work that started early and ended late you are exhausted. The boss chewed you out in front of all your coworkers. A customer screamed his displeasure in your ear so emphatically it's still ringing. And there wasn't time for lunch, so you haven't had a thing to eat since that banana you grabbed as you flew out the door this morning.

As you step from your car, lugging behind you a bulging briefcase with reports that have to be reviewed before tomorrow's big meeting, your youngest child hurtles herself at your midsection. She's wailing about the toy her brother "deliberately" broke. You attempt to soothe her while dragging both of you into the house.

Your spouse is standing in the kitchen taking inventory of the dinner possibilities with a look of such exhaustion and frustration on his face that it can be matched only by your own. As your son sails down the hallway on his skateboard, throwing insults over his shoulder at his sister, the dog presents himself at your feet. Relieved to be greeted by a friendly face you reach down to rub his ear. He responds by throwing up pizza and Gummi Bears all over your new shoes.

In the midst of this chaos, the doorbell rings. You and your spouse exchange "Now what?" looks. Stepping out of your shoes, you walk to the door, ready to unload your frustrations on the salesperson you suspect is on the other side. After you jerk the door open, you are surprised to see a woman in a flowing blue robe standing before you.

"Is this the Smith residence?" she asks, reading from a sheet of paper and then peering up at you over the top of her glasses.

"Yes," you reply, drawing the word out as if it had ten syllables rather than one. Quickly, you scan your peripheral vision for men carrying cameras or a van with CANDID CAMERA stenciled on the side.

"Well, then, this is your lucky day!" she proclaims, letting her glasses drop and swing from the chain around her neck. Shoving the piece of paper up one sleeve, she pulls a golden wand from the other. "I am your vacation fairy godmother. You have won an all-expense-paid trip anywhere in the world you'd like to go. Just name the destination of your choice and I'll zap you there myself."

You can hear your family gathering behind you. As they murmur their curiosity, you try to find an intelligible reply to voice. But all that comes out is "Yeah, right."

"Tsk, tsk, tsk," your fairy godmother chastises. Muttering about never being believed, she points her wand at the shrub next to the door frame. A bolt of electricity shoots out, transforming the plant into a suitcase. Your children shriek with delight.

"Voilà!" she says, with a grand flourish of her arm. "Now do you believe me?"

"Ah . . . well . . . yes," you sputter.

"Great. Now let's see if we can't find something to eat. I'm starved." She pushes her way past you and disappears in the direction of the kitchen, yelling over her shoulder, "Just let me know what you decide."

You stand there, incredulous, glancing between your equally surprised spouse and the form fading down the hallway. As your children cautiously creep after her, the two of you are left standing alone. "Well, where do we want to go?" you finally ask.

WHERE WOULD *you* want to go? If there were no limitations, such as time or money, where would you choose to travel? How long would you be gone? What route would you take? Would you go alone or with someone else?

While our chosen destinations and itineraries may be as variable as our personalities, I think there would be some fairly common themes in what we want to achieve on our dream vacation. Some may select a leisurely excursion to the most beautiful beaches in the world, while others would line up a cycling tour of the great castles of Europe. But I believe we would all seek to be revitalized and renewed by our experience. We want an adventure that will transform our lives in whatever way we most need it to be transformed.

Perhaps you want to calm your stressed psyche, restore balance to your life, or reignite the passion in your romance. There may be a sight you've always wanted to see or a trek you've always wanted to make that you know will help define your vision and purpose in life. You may be searching for the one thing that will fill the emptiness inside you or answer a question that has rattled around inside your soul for years.

If any of these sound like purposes you would want your dream vacation to meet, then you are reading the right book. Making a journey to the River of Truth—the source of universal wisdom—will do all those things and more. You might be headed to a different geographic point along the river from other travelers or use a different mode of transportation from others who make the voyage. Yet because we are all seeking essentially the same things, the process will be similar. We want to deepen and broaden our connection with Spirit, others, and ourselves through the creation of a sacred text that reflects our unique relationship with her. Capturing our story is important because we know there never has been, and never will be, another one exactly like it. We know that if we avoid this journey we cheat ourselves, Spirit, and the universe out of a richer experience. So, after careful consideration, you have decided that the River of Truth is your ideal vacation destination. Having a solid grounding in the concepts involved in creating your personal sacred text from your journey to the River of Truth is very important. It will help you stay focused through the lengthy process and prevent you from getting lost along the way. It's hard to prepare for a journey if you do not know its nature. Therefore, we'll stop here and take a few moments to define exactly what a personal sacred text is by looking at each term, separately and together.

Personal

ACCORDING TO MOST dictionary definitions, "personal" means individual, private, and having to do with characteristics of being a human being. For our purposes we won't stray too far from these definitions. In the context of creating a sacred text, the word "personal" has three meanings: individual, unique, and dynamic.

Compiling a volume of work that reflects your spiritual beliefs and experiences is a very *individual* undertaking. Although you may be used to a faith tradition that values the collective experience and process, reflected in community worship services and governed by dogma and doctrine, this particular process is about your own differentiated values, beliefs, and ideas. It is not about what anyone else thinks or feels unless that is germane to your arriving at a particular thought of your own. It is not about the blind recitation of catechism or the mindless regurgitation of facts and stories you learned as a child. When you hold your sacred text up to a mirror, you want to see your own reflection, not the "should," "ought," or "must" interpretations of anyone else.

This process is about you and your journey. It is your story of the explorations and discoveries you have made, and still want to make, about Spirit and yourself. If, in the process, you decide to own someone else's beliefs because they adequately reflect your own, that's great! The goal is to avoid adopting ideals incongruent with who you are.

Although this is a sacred text you are making solely for yourself, there may be a time, during or after its creation, that you decide to share some or all of it with a trusted friend or family member. The decision is entirely up to you, and chapter 15 will help you with that process. Despite the deeply personal nature of their texts, all of my clients and workshop participants have chosen to share at least small pieces of them with others or to leave their entire texts to loved ones after their deaths. For this reason, it is important to consider potential readers when you are creating your text. It need not be a primary or significant focus, but if you wish to share your story with anyone in the world, you should consider whether it will be understood clearly. Therefore, you will see many references in this book about "readers" of your personal sacred text. Incorporate the related suggestions as appropriate to your particular desires for sharing your text.

Creating a sacred text is also a *unique* process. There never has been, and there never will be, another human being exactly like you. Your thoughts, personality, ideas, and behaviors will go unduplicated for all of time. Consequently, no one has or ever will again have the understanding of and relationship with Spirit that you do. Your work will have a value unequal to anything else that will ever be done.

In making your selections and writing your scripture, seek to reveal your uniqueness. Boldly declare what makes you who you are, how you are different from everyone else, and what transpired in your life to create your unparalleled relationship with Spirit. Celebrate your separateness from the rest of humanity! Give the universe the gift of knowing who you are so we can all learn from your experience.

Your personal sacred text should reflect the *dynamic* quality of your human life. None of us is stagnant. Even if we choose to dig our heels into the dirt as hard as we can, circumstances eventually will dislodge us, dragging us into growth and change. We can embrace this or fight it, but we cannot avoid it.

Over the years as you grow and change, your sacred text, whether you intend it or not, will reflect the dynamic nature of your evolving beliefs and spiritual ideals. You may wish to make your evolution a conscious part of the story you tell. Or you may simply prefer to let it unfold on its own, an ever-flowing undercurrent in your journey to the River of Truth. The choice is yours. My only suggestion is that you welcome the evolution as a part of the process rather than choose rigidity or constancy.

Sacred

THIS WORD IS a little trickier to define, primarily because in different spiritual traditions it has various meanings. For some it encompasses a very broad category of ideas, actions, or places that are concerned with divinity. For others it designates something that is so holy that it is unmentionable or inviolable. While you will have to be the ultimate judge for where you wish to draw the line, I lean toward the comprehensive rather than the exclusive interpretation. After all, if something is so sacred that it's unmentionable, how could we undertake writing about it in a productive manner?

In the context of our work, the word "sacred" will be liberally defined as anything relating to Spirit. Using this terminology will give you as much freedom as you need to open your soul to a world of possibilities. Will you find that a comic strip has a sacred meaning? Can you see a part of a movie as having a profound spiritual message? Allow this definition to guide you into new areas of spiritual exploration as well as into those you have previously trod, as you consider what to include in your personal sacred text.

Text

THIS WORD USUALLY refers to a written volume of work. Typically, it is associated with a more scholarly or academic book. For instance, you would rarely settle into a lounge chair at poolside and ask the fellow next to you, "What John Grisham text are you reading?" On the other hand, you wouldn't hesitate to commiserate with a fellow student over the high price of the texts for the coming semester.

For our purposes, I think the best definition of "text" is: a carefully constructed record comprised mainly of the written word. When you see that a personal sacred text can include sheet music, photographs, or even small objects that represent something especially meaningful, you will appreciate the broad interpretation.

Personal Sacred Text

FOR A MOMENT, let's look at how our definitions for the words in this phrase come together. If "personal" means individual, unique, and dynamic; "sacred" refers to things relating to Spirit; and "text" means a carefully constructed record primarily in a written form, then what is a personal sacred text? I think one of the best clarifying definitions I have ever read comes from Huston Smith's *Illustrated World's Religions*. Although he is referring specifically to sacred art, I think his words can easily include the personal sacred text as an art form:

> *Mention of vision is important here. . . . What makes art sacred is not what it depicts, but the way it opens onto transcendence and carries the viewer with it, enabling him or her to see what it might be like to live in self-forgetfulness and timeless harmony.*

For me, the key element of Smith's definition is his description of how sacred art opens a window onto a dimension of the world seen by the artist. This means, of course, that every piece is a unique reflection of its creator's interpretation of spirituality—one that every viewer of that work is not going to necessarily agree with. But for some, it will turn on a light that illuminates their path. In that instant the artist, the viewer, and Spirit will become one.

Using Smith's concept and my own experiences with this process, I have arrived at a working definition of the phrase "personal sacred text." I conceive of it as a volume of work that creates a triangular relationship among the writer, the reader, and Spirit with the apex of the triangle pointing toward Spirit. Your personal sacred text is a creation that reflects your unique, individual, and dynamic relationship with Spirit. If people were to read your text, they would be transported into your view on the spiritual realm. Through your eyes they would see Spirit and what she means in your life. They would experience your journey to the River of Truth.

That doesn't mean they have to agree with you or even completely understand your work. Neither agreement nor understanding is a prerequisite to their seeing, even for a very brief moment, a glimpse of how you see the world. Your work will be a lens focusing readers' sight through your soul and onto a vision of Spirit—nothing more, but absolutely nothing less.

Putting It All Together

YOUR PERSONAL sacred text is comprised of two things: material created by others and your own scripture writing. The subject matter is of your own choosing, concentrating on issues and themes central to your life. The type of material can vary widely, from poetry, to song lyrics, to sections of a screenplay. You may choose selections from sacred texts already in existence or write your own essay if you can't find something that captures exactly what you want to say. There are very few limits and lots of room to explore.

As you have been reading, perhaps you are thinking of including in your text a particular piece of work that you have read before. If so, that's great. If not, that's all right. Give yourself some time to read the next few chapters and develop a better idea of what a personal sacred text is all about. By the time you get to the reviews of the sacred and secular literature and the discussion of different forms of scripture you could write yourself, I guarantee you'll have an idea for where you want to begin your journey.

TWO

The Rewards of Creating a Personal Sacred Text

HERE IS A MOMENT in the planning of any project when you consider the benefits of undertaking it. Will it be worth your time and effort? Are there going to be enough positive outcomes? To answer these questions you do some research and analyze the pros and cons. Making the decision to create your personal sacred text is no different.

After reading the first chapter you are undoubtedly thinking something like "This is going to take some work, maybe even some hard work." You're right. It is going to require an investment of your time, effort, and emotional, spiritual, and intellectual energy. There will be moments when things don't go your way or the process seems stuck. If you make the decision on whether to create a personal sacred text based solely on ease, then you probably will put this book down right about now. But you do not yet have the largest chunk of information that will weigh heavily against those factors: the rewards of creating your personal sacred text.

Creating a personal sacred text is a powerful, transformative process. Every ounce of time and energy you invest in it will be returned to you many times over. You will receive, in return, far-reaching benefits that will impact your relationship with yourself, Spirit, and others. Let's take the time to look at the specific rewards that fall into each of these three categories.

Relationship with Self

CREATING YOUR PERSONAL sacred text will invite you to encounter traditions and beliefs that are unfamiliar and perhaps even initially unappealing to you. You may have never considered reading about the Hindu faith. Perhaps you will read the Buddhist sacred texts and encounter beliefs you had either never previously considered or had dismissed as incongruent with your understanding of Spirit. You may stumble across or purposely seek out an answer to a spiritual conundrum you had been struggling with and be surprised to find it in a faith that is new to you. The concept of writing your own scripture may be foreign to you.

All of these explorations will cause your perspective on life to stretch and expand. While the world will not change, the way you see it will. The longer you search, the more comfortable you will find yourself feeling in new and unusual circumstances. Gradually, your receptiveness to ideas and beliefs will increase, allowing you to experience that mystical interaction with Spirit. There will be an emotional, spiritual, and intellectual interchange between you and the places you encounter. You may not walk away from each meeting having adopted the beliefs held there, but you will not leave unaffected.

With every step of your journey, you will be changed. As you look for answers, ideas, clarification, and validation, not only will you learn more about the places you visit, but you will gain greater awareness of yourself. From each stage in the process, from deciding where to go to what you will look for, you will gain greater self-understanding. It's an unavoidable result of your journey.

One of the greatest searches involved in the creation of my personal sacred text was for answers to my questions about suffering. I couldn't even begin, though, without first deciding what my current beliefs were. Then I had to figure out why what I had already explored was not providing me with the information I sought.

Solid in my belief that my past did not hold the answers, I made a few initial forays into traditions other than those I had been raised with. I chose to examine several Eastern philosophies because they were, I ignorantly believed, radically different from what I knew. As I explored I looked for indications that within that belief system I would find something more congruent with my experience. The process of examining something new stretched the limitations of my tolerance and judgment and brought to light prejudices within me that I didn't know existed.

From my childhood I had been taught that belief in anything other than Christianity earned one nothing other than a straight passage to hell. Although no one ever gave me much of an explanation for why that was so, they did set up clear rules and regulations for seeking my own answers. I found a very tall and rigid fence set at the edge of the Christian faith, electrified with a current of damnation. As a result, I had bought into the prejudice that everything outside the boundary was wrong without supporting evidence. I even joined in the bigotry, proclaiming non-Christians to be on the wrong path. But I always felt righteous in my statements because I had been taught that they were just.

It was not until I started crossing the boundaries and studying other spiritual traditions that I recognized my beliefs as sheer and unwarranted prejudice. Instead of magic and hocus-pocus based on pure fiction, I found great wisdom in other spiritual traditions. I did not agree with everything, but then I was no longer completely sold on what my own religion had taught me either. There was a great richness there, along with a very valuable lesson.

Once I crossed that hurdle, I had to test my initial explorations for their fit with my experience. This required more self-examination to clarify again what I believed and why something did or did not fit. Gradually my ideas became more defined, my research was increasing in productivity, and my pace was becoming quicker. It was like moving from quicksand to mud with a consistency thick enough to allow me finally to gain ground.

After identifying several beliefs with potential for holding my truth, I embarked on a voyage deep into their territory. The searching not only challenged my previous beliefs but also clarified the new ones I was building. My confidence grew as I gained a greater understanding of who I was and where I was headed.

When I finally arrived at a satisfactory destination, I found that I not only had the answers I sought, but I also had an increased awareness and appreciation of myself. I had come such a long way and was proud of myself for having negotiated the journey. Additionally, I now had a new belief that was founded on my own search and struggle rather than on doctrine.

You will gain self-awareness and understanding with every adventure in the process of creating your personal sacred text. Every step that you take will give you clarity and affirmation about who you are and whether you are headed in the right direction or need to turn onto a different path. Without this increasing insight you will not be able to proceed in creating your personal sacred text. It is a process that cannot be separated from the rest of your voyage.

As you grow to know yourself better, clarifying beliefs that you currently hold or replacing old ideas that are no longer useful, you will find your self-esteem improving. Happily, this is unavoidable. You are building a life and relationship with Spirit that is tailored to match you perfectly. It is based on no one's demands or expectations other than your own. How could that not be affirming and encouraging to your self-concept? And as you find a greater love for yourself, you will discover a heightened capacity to love others, including Spirit.

Through these gains in understanding and caring for yourself you will likely find the power to heal wounds and difficulties in your life. Although this is not a guaranteed result of creating your personal sacred text, if you commit yourself to the process wholeheartedly the likelihood of encountering the miracle of healing somewhere in your journey is extremely high.

My clients and workshop participants have found amazing power to overcome difficulties in their lives when they undertook the process of creating their personal sacred text. The spiritual discoveries they made and the self-esteem they gained was healing in ways standard therapy had not been.

Sharon, an alcoholic who struggled to become sober for years, found a new relationship with Spirit by creating her personal sacred text. She was able to forgive herself for marital infidelities she had committed long ago. As she became more merciful with herself, she was able to let go of other long-harbored hurts and expectations. Secure for the first time in a relationship with a loving Spirit and herself, she was finally able to walk away from her addiction to alcohol.

I worked for several months with another client, a man with a history of domestic violence, in an effort to create his personal sacred text. Ben brutally beat his wife, Mary—at times to the point of unconsciousness. He was preparing to go to trial on his third assault charge and faced years of jail time. As we explored his Islamic faith, Ben was reluctant to read any material that did not originate in his spiritual tradition. I encouraged him to explore the poetry of the Sufi masters, who are Islamic mystics. Although the Qur'an has many passages that discuss love of self and others, Ben had not been able to make a spiritual connection with it. In the wonderful, lyrical love poetry of the Sufis, though, he finally was able to embrace a gentler relationship with himself, his god, and his wife. Although it was not a cure, it did open the door for us to do some amazing healing work in his anger management and his marriage.

The examination, discovery, and openness to inviting Spirit into your life more fully are powerful conductors of the kind of energy that resolves the pain of the past and present. I have seen it happen time and time again. My clients have seen remarkable healing in relationships, experienced an end to debilitating mental illness, and found the power to halt the cycle of addictions due to their creation of a personal sacred text. The power is there for you too.

Relationship with Spirit

CREATING A PERSONAL sacred text will transform the way you practice your spirituality. This is a natural outgrowth of the personal changes you will experience during the process. As you become more aware of yourself, you will find ways to express your faith that are ideally suited to who you are and what you believe. After all, when you are unsure of your form of worship, it's much easier to take someone else's advice about the ideal spiritual practice. It would be something like going shopping for a suit without knowing your size and trusting that the salesperson could guess it by looking at you. No one can decide the best way for you to relate to Spirit except you.

By creating your personal sacred text, you will gain the self-awareness to realize how poorly past spiritual practices may have addressed your needs. As I progressed through this process, I realized how ill-fitting my practice of reciting memorized prayers was to fostering my spiritual growth. You will be able to let go of things that no longer fit you and explore to the ends of the earth for a method of communing with Spirit and living your beliefs that is exactly tailored to you. Or if your beliefs and practices were working for you, you will understand why they work and can make adjustments necessary to gain maximum results. You may find a method of prayer or meditation that fits you perfectly or perhaps a devotion or ritual that will allow you to convey exactly the song of your heart unlike anything else ever could. As you discover and put these practices into motion, you will find the results so satisfying because they are perfectly suited to your needs and personality that you are motivated to engage in them again and again.

These practices, along with the increase in your personal awareness and self-esteem, will produce a relationship with Spirit that is broader and deeper than you have ever experienced. I had no idea how narrow and shallow my ideas about Spirit were before I embarked on my journey to the River of Truth. In hindsight, given the culture in which I was raised and my lack of experience with other spiritual traditions, I understand why. But my narrow definitions never would have expanded had I not begun searching in other spiritual traditions and taking the risk to open myself up to new ideas and beliefs.

As I found new and healthy concepts of Spirit, my relationship with him exploded in all directions. No longer was my present or future limited by the past. As you grow to understand and love yourself, find new ways to commune with Spirit, and build a belief system that is based on your unique experience, you will also find your relationship with Spirit altered in a radical and positive way. Your new interactions with him will bring you increased power, love, and wisdom.

Relationship with Others

YOUR INCREASED ABILITY to love yourself and Spirit will result in a greater capacity to love others. The energy behind love is one that naturally re-creates itself wherever it goes. As others receive your gift, they will experience a greater capacity to return it to you, thus completing the cycle.

I've lost count of the number of times that, as a client and a therapist, I have heard it preached that you cannot expect others to care for you if you do not first care about yourself. I believe there is truth to that statement, but only if you invert it. There is little validity to the idea that we are lovable only to the extent that we can love ourselves. This idea is contrary to the teachings of almost every spiritual tradition in the world, which teach that we have value and are worthy of unconditional love simply because we exist. I have found that after we have learned to love ourselves without condition, we easily extend that same gift to others. It is not that we were incapable of doing so before, but our capacity to do so for everyone we meet increases exponentially after we know how to do it for ourselves.

Your relationships with others will improve in many ways as you journey to the River of Truth. Your partner, children, coworkers, and friends will all benefit from your journey. As they experience more love from you, they in turn will be better able to love themselves and others. Creating a personal sacred text is a gift that extends beyond yourself into every corner of the world you touch.

While the possibilities for impacting the greater community with the fruits of your work are endless, one has such potential that it warrants being addressed separately. Creating a personal sacred text can have a powerful impact on your acceptance of other faith traditions—something our world has struggled with since time began. Intolerance of those different from us is at the root of virtually every war, genocide, and terrorist attack around the world. Narrowly defined concepts of who and what is acceptable drive us to commit terrible atrocities over and over again.

I am not proposing that world peace would reign if everyone undertook to create a personal sacred text. But I do believe that each of us can increase our knowledge and acceptance of others through our personal journey. As you study sacred literature and practices from around the world with an increasingly open mind, you will acquire an understanding of them. You may never adopt them as your own, but you will develop a respect for them that goes a long way toward acceptance. It isn't enough that you settle for tolerating them. Work until you can believe that for the followers of that faith, those beliefs are correct and good. Give them the same right to choose how they will define and relate to Spirit as you would hope they give to you. As you grow in your ability to love yourself without limit, you will find this part of the journey easier and immensely rewarding.

ALTHOUGH IT IS highly likely that the first rewards will be personal when creating your sacred text, then extend to Spirit and others, there are no hard-and-fast rules. Growth in the personal realm can trigger forward movement in relationships with others. Your growth can supply motivation and energy to another area, as if they were linked by the flow of electrical current.

As a marriage and family therapist I work with interconnecting relationships on a daily basis. I typically spend the first few sessions with my clients explaining what the therapeutic community refers to as "the family system." In layman's terms, this means that each individual person's movement does not occur in a vacuum but instead impacts the rest of the family members. When Mom gets a job after being at home for a decade, everyone feels the change. Chores are adjusted, new rituals are established, budgets get rearranged, and everyone has to get used to Mom's new schedule and absence. A divorce rocks the lives of not only the couple involved but the children and extended family members as well.

When you throw a rock into the water, ripples travel across the entire lake. The ripples may diminish in magnitude as they go, but even the final, faintest ripple has some impact. Changes you make in the process of creating your personal sacred text will follow the same pattern. While they may begin in one area, eventually they will result in movement throughout your life.

These changes will likely occur in a cyclical manner. An issue you thought you had resolved permanently will surface again. Don't be surprised. Instead take careful note of how it is different this time around. Chances are high that although it is the same issue, it will not be an exact duplicate of what you had tackled in the past (unless you're in denial about truly having resolved it). This time it will show itself on a deeper level or founded in a different context. For example, you may have resolved your trust issues concerning your relationship with Spirit only to be confronted years later with similar problems in the area of friendships with the opposite sex.

Personally and professionally, I have found that we tend to travel through life in an upward spiral, repeatedly moving through the same challenges but on an increasingly higher level. Do not be dismayed if this seems to be happening for you. It is almost always *not* a sign that you are not making progress. Take some time to stop and assess where you really are, then move on, confident that you are being guided on exactly the path you need to be traveling.

While the benefits of relationships with self, Spirit, and others as a result of creating your personal sacred text are positive, they also can be unsettling and perhaps overwhelming. Take care of yourself on this journey. Frequent breaks are encouraged and necessary. Above all, don't let any discomfort with the exercise of creating your personal sacred text drive you to force a specific issue to resolution or abandon the journey all together. As you progress, you will grow accustomed to the process and learn successful ways of coping with the resulting changes. Use those lessons as fuel for guiding further study and fodder for your personal scripture writing.

THREE

The Process of Creating Your Personal Sacred Text

SUMMER CAMPING VACATIONS were a regular part of my childhood. A consistent part of that tradition was obtaining a trip planning kit from the local automobile club. Several weeks before we were set to depart, Mom and I would go down to their offices with our instructions detailing which route we'd chosen to take and which campgrounds we'd decided to visit. I stood at the counter watching them chart our travels on tall, skinny sections of maps that they assembled into a booklet held together with a plastic comb binding. During the trip I found great delight in watching Mom fold over each section as she navigated us through the book. I studied the details of each page, committing the roads, cities, and side trips to memory. Knowing that information gave me a sense of excitement and a feeling of security.

Mapping your process of creating a personal sacred text before you even begin has a similar benefit, especially if this kind of journey is new to you. You already know your general destination, but there are many routes to get there and various ways to travel each path. Once you make your first foray into the extensive collections of sacred and secular literature and into the various ways to write your own scripture, you will find extensive avenues to explore. In fact, the options are so numerous that beginning without some sort of a plan will likely result in your becoming overwhelmed and confused before you get too far. So let's stop for a moment and examine your options, review what routes others have found successful, and discuss what you can expect to encounter along the way.

Where Can I Look for Selections and Inspiration?

THE RIVER OF TRUTH flows underneath every possible source—from the sacred texts of the world's religions to secular sources such as comic strips and screenplays. But in order to recognize the wisdom everywhere you go, you need to look with an open mind that is earnestly seeking to encounter it. Many of us were never taught how to cultivate such an attitude of receptive seeking. Fewer of us have had many opportunities to practice using it.

Consequently you may not be able to locate spiritual wisdom in what are traditionally seen as secular materials. For this reason you will start reviewing resources in those places wisdom is easiest to find, amid sacred literature like the Christian Bible and the Hindu Upanishads, allowing you the time to develop your detection and exploration skills. Then you will ease your way into more challenging and remote resources, such as essays and poetry, where you will have many opportunities to further refine your ability to detect the presence of wisdom. By this time you will have developed skill in locating Spirit in *every* source.

Finally you will move into the completely uncharted territory of writing your own scripture. All of the skills you have developed and all of the knowledge you have obtained to this point will be put to use as you record your thoughts, beliefs, and experiences in your own words.

For the first time you will be able to see your progress in evaluating, exploring, and expanding your understanding of and relationship with Spirit take shape using your own voice. Ideas and beliefs that you had not realized were percolating inside you will be brought to light. Growth you did not know had occurred will be revealed, and vague concepts will be clarified.

Once you have followed the initial sequence—exploring sacred texts, then more secular sources, and finally writing your own scripture—you will have developed enough skill and familiarity with the process to be able to weave back and forth between them according to your need. For example, reading a section of the Tao Te Ching will spark an idea that leads you to explore the writings of Ursula Le Guin. From there you may decide to write your first poem about what you've learned. Or perhaps you'll journal about the new ideas you're exploring as you turn to the writings of Confucius. You will be limited only by your comfort with the process and the time you have available.

How Long Will the Process Take?

YOUR EXPLORATION of the River of Truth will take as long as you wish. The time frame for your process is entirely up to you. In determining how much time you wish to invest in creating your text, remember that the amount of energy you put into it will largely determine the extent of the rewards you will gain. A sacred text compiled over the course of three weeks will not have nearly the impact on your life as the one you take three months to complete.

Although creating your personal sacred text is not a process that will take a lifetime, it is not a simple or superficial one either. Often it requires in-depth study of your own beliefs along with those of others. It will involve self-examination and inquiry. Not all of your questions will have easy answers; some may require research into areas you had previously not explored. Throughout this process things will happen in your life to change your perspective or cause you to rethink an idea you had previously held as rock solid. Those events may change the nature and tone of your sacred text. Use your life experiences to enrich the process of creating your text.

For example, you might hear a presentation at a professional conference that sparks an idea. On the airplane headed home an essay flows from your pen. A few weeks later you are watching a movie in the theater and the main character says a line that makes you sit bolt upright in your chair. It is so clearly congruent with something you had been thinking for years but could not articulate yourself that you scribble it on a napkin in the dark. Much of your progress will be serendipitous like this, rather than planned and calculated.

You will begin creating your text the moment you make your first selection and can continue to add to it for as long as you wish. Although it will be in various stages of formation for a long time, at each stage it is completely usable for enriching your spiritual life. Do not rush through the completion process just to be able to enjoy the finished product. The process needs time to mature and develop at its own pace. If you hurry it, you will be cheating yourself because the final product will have significantly less power than it would if it were allowed time to grow to its complete breadth and depth.

Just because your personal sacred text will be completed over a significant length of time, it is not a mammoth project that will consume large quantities of your time. There may be months when you do not make any additions to your text. At other times you may seem to be adding something every day. That ebb and flow is to be expected and is consistent with the type of project you are undertaking. I estimate that my clients and I spend an average of three to four hours a week working on our texts after the initial stage of learning the process. That initial stage may require more time, perhaps five to seven hours a week for a month or two.

Should I Work Alone or with Others?

ALTHOUGH THERE MAY BE moments when you will encounter a fellow sacred text creator headed in the same direction as you, the creation of a personal sacred text is mostly a solitary journey. You may choose to share your progress, lessons, trials, selections, and writing with someone else, but because this is such an individualized process, joining with someone else for the work involved will only cheat you out of an experience that is tailored to your specific needs and desires. We are all unique creatures with experiences, thoughts, and beliefs that will combine to drive our explorations in a way that cannot be the same as anyone else's. Adjusting your journey to accommodate someone else will only detract from the power of the process for both of you.

I understand that, for some, the idea of undertaking this journey alone is frightening, especially if it is a new and unfamiliar concept. If this is the case for you, I recommend you find a friend or group of friends to share your experiences with on a formal or informal basis. Chapter 15 will give you a variety of ideas and options for sharing your process of creating a personal sacred text with others.

During one of my workshops I noticed that two women were spending all of their breaks huddled together in the back of the room. I knew they had not been acquainted prior to our group meetings. Curious, I approached them and saw that they were furiously reading pages from each other's texts. Spotting me, they rushed to explain that they had discovered during a group exercise that they shared remarkably similar spiritual journeys and had struck up an immediate kinship. They provided each other with much more encouragement and support that weekend than I ever could have. Six years later they are still keeping up with each other's progress via e-mail.

Are There Rules and Guidelines I Need to Follow?

THANKFULLY, your journey to the River of Truth comes with very few rules. Although the process does not necessarily qualify as being called carefree, because of the challenging personal work involved, it is relatively limitation free. You can progress at your own pace, using any resources you wish, explore any school or thought or spiritual tradition that you choose, and voice any thoughts or feelings that come into your mind.

I will offer you a variety of options and suggestions for your process, based on my years of experience, but the final choices are up to you. Developing hard-and-fast rules would imply that I believe I know what is best for every reader. I don't know, and would not presume to guess, what is the best method for you to use in creating your sacred text. Only you know that. Your journey will be as personal as your sacred text.

Initially having such freedom may be scary. Over time that fear will transform into a passion to explore the world with abandon. Allow yourself the time to move from being unfamiliar with having no limits to being motivated by the opportunities it provides. In the beginning you may wish to follow these few simple guidelines to steer you on your way:

1. Dedicate a specific amount of time to creating your personal sacred text, perhaps one hour a day or one afternoon a week. Protect that time by scheduling it into your calendar like an appointment.

2. Start searching for selections from material that you are familiar with. For example, if your faith background is Jewish, begin reviewing the Talmud and the Torah for excerpts that you know are particularly meaningful. As you get the hang

of making selections and adding them to your text, you can expand into new areas.

3. Use the highest-quality resources you can find. Seek out the most accurate translations and the most current materials. Always look for a complete text rather than an abridged format, if available.

4. Persevere through the rough spots. A wonderful Chinese proverb says: "You can only go halfway into the darkest forest. Then you are coming out the other side."

5. Be as flexible as possible and open to new ideas.

6. Expand your boundaries. Look outside the faith of your childhood and adulthood. Try a taste of something new before you reject it entirely.

7. Use every aspect of your life as food for thought in making selections and writing scripture. Don't try to focus on just "spiritual" moments.

8. Write scripture based on your own experiences. Avoid writing about a friend's spiritual journey or the lesson a peer learned while exploring a spiritual tradition. Your scripture should focus on *your* process, not that of others.

9. Ask for help and feedback from those around you, preferably individuals who are also creating a sacred text, but at least those who are sympathetic to your undertaking.

10. If you feel stuck or immobilized, change directions. Let a completely new idea refresh your mind and renew your journey.

This Is a Mystical Journey

WHILE IN TODAY'S SOCIETY the term "mystic" usually brings to mind images of a spiritual extremist only partially anchored in reality, an accurate definition couldn't be more different. A mystic is one who interacts with reality by living in it rather than viewing it from an elevated platform of a purely rational perspective. Mystics seek a balance of spiritual, emotional, and intellectual experience. Their intuition, rather than their analytical minds, guides them. Although you may not consider yourself a mystic, this journey will have mystical qualities. As you seek to immerse yourself in what you read and write rather than simply to observe with your intellect, you'll also observe with your heart.

This is the primary reason that prior knowledge of sacred texts and literature is not necessary for creating a personal sacred text. Neither is it important to be highly educated or even that you consider yourself "smart." This journey is not made with your intellect but with your mystical intuition. The aim is not to fill your head with more knowledge about Spirit or to arrive at ideas and beliefs via logical analysis. Ironically, to do so will actually drive you farther away from your goal of enjoying a greater understanding of and relationship with Spirit. The deeper you sink into a purely intellectual analysis, the farther you move from a balanced and total experience.

In the Hindu tradition there are four paths to reaching union with Spirit, which is believed to be the primary goal of human existence. The four methods, called *yogas*, are knowledge, love, work, and psychophysical exercise. The path of knowledge, bhakti yoga, is believed to be the most direct. This is the road you will be taking. It is important to realize that, in Hinduism, knowledge does not refer to intellectual or factual information. Instead it is understood to be an intuitive perception that has a transformative power. As believers acquire greater and greater discernment, they come to resemble that which they are seeking to understand.

The creation of a personal sacred text has a similar power because it is also a mystical process. As you progress, you will interact with what you encounter on every possible level. The intellectual, emotional, and spiritual experiences integrate the material into your life and into your selections and writing in ways that you cannot begin to imagine. The longer you remain true to the mystical journey, the more closely you will find your life conforming to the ideal existence you see.

This Is an Empowering Journey

CREATING A PERSONAL sacred text is a self-perpetuating process. Starting requires an initial investment of motivation and time, but, once begun, the adventure fuels itself. The validation received from discovering and writing material that echoes your understanding of life results in a new vibrancy in your attitude. Clarification of your ideas and beliefs through exploration leads to a renewed sense of purpose. Old, unhealthy beliefs are erased and replaced with healthy ideals; breaking the strong ties of the past frees all the energy that was required to maintain those connections. As you create your text and conform more closely to your ideal self, your confidence and feeling of worth soar. You can direct the resulting energy into creating a better life and continuing the journey that has garnered such wonderful benefits.

Having grown up with the idea that Spirit expected nothing less than perfection from me, I never felt like I measured up to her expectations. One evening I picked up Alan Cohen's book *The Dragon Doesn't Live Here Anymore* and began reading it. Suddenly all of the pieces fell into place. I finally realized I was good enough, right here and right now, with no additional improvement necessary to earn the love I desired. An incredible energy exploded inside my body. I felt like Superman, able to leap tall buildings in a single bound. I immediately went into my bathroom and wrote "I am good enough" on the mirror in lipstick. It's still there today, reminding me of a powerful breakthrough and the power it freed within me.

I often use the analogy of a jigsaw puzzle when explaining the concept of creating a personal sacred text. When you begin a puzzle, an initial anticipatory excitement gives you the energy to tackle the mundane task of setting the pieces out right side up. Once you begin to connect them and see the picture emerge, a whole new motivation kicks in that only increases as you progress. It is an empowering process because you watch the finished product form before your eyes.

This Is a Dynamic Journey

THIS IS NOT a static journey. Just as your life is changed by what you encounter along the way, so will your personal sacred text be influenced. You will undoubtedly be surprised or captivated by something you see, read, or hear during your process that causes you to change directions. Although you may have intended to research Hinduism, Buddhism may distract you. Perhaps you will experience a great tragedy or make a personal breakthrough that renders the idea you were chasing moot. For example, trying to find a poem to express the joy you felt when you met Spirit during a peaceful sunrise may become meaningless when you discover a piece to the puzzle of why your mom was taken from you by death when you were so young.

Jim came into my office one morning muttering about "moving targets." When I asked him what he meant, he complained at length about having to rewrite the table of contents for his personal sacred text once again, although he had already done so numerous times. He kept finding new pieces that radically altered the order and tone of his text. He thought he was doing something wrong. After we talked about how such changes are a part of the process, he decided to forgo the table of contents until his text was finished.

All of this is not only okay, it's to be expected. Because creating a personal sacred text mirrors your life so closely, you will not be able to avoid interruptions in the process. It's fine to plan ahead, but try to remain as flexible as possible while you're carrying out your plans. Do not resist change. Seek to learn how to move with the ebb and flow of your life rather than against it.

This Is a Challenging Journey

THE PROCESS OF CREATING your personal sacred text includes varying levels of difficulty. At times it will be as easy as finding the exact translation of the I Ching you were looking for on your first trip to the bookstore. Or it may be as hard as the very next day trying to write a poem and succeeding only in staring at a blank sheet of paper for hours with absolutely no words coming into your head. You will have control over most of the choices that lead you into gentler or more difficult processes, but some challenges will come as a complete surprise.

It is important to remember that challenge is not negative. It provides powerful energy for encouraging personal growth. But it will require that you face some difficulties and allow yourself to be stretched in new directions. You may encounter beliefs or ideals in a particular spiritual tradition that cause you to feel uncomfortable because they are a radical departure from what you hold true or because you may have always been taught that they were wrong or bad. You will feel your world expanding as you push yourself to the limit of what you previously knew to be the edge of existence.

As a therapist I see many clients come through my door because they have encountered a crisis. For some reason or another their world has been rocked to the core. It feels disastrous and often they wonder if they can survive. But with support and encouragement, they eventually find enough stability to stop, look around, and assess their situation. Then they can make healthy decisions on how to handle the crisis in the best possible manner. Over time they arrive at the other side of the crisis and realize how much they have changed and grown as a result of the challenges they faced. That does not mean they would want to repeat the process—and I never propose to people that they seek out a crisis just to achieve personal growth—but they have found a blessing in the midst of their pain and struggle.

Your journey may have some of the same qualities. While trying to write a story about a childhood event, you may uncover disturbing memories that you had not previously recalled. As you read love poetry, you are confronted with the damage the affair you had several years ago wreaked on your marriage. Perhaps all your life you thought you had an accurate conception of what it means to be a child of Spirit, but then you encounter an obscure passage in another spiritual tradition that makes a solid case for a completely contrary belief. All of these instances would result in some significant soul-searching, questioning, and reevaluating. While none may be particularly pleasant in the moment, the chances that each will result in positive change are extremely high—if you let them work for you.

As a society we are conditioned to believe that stress is bad. We take classes on how to manage our stress and talk about Type A personalities as if they were flawed. But it is very important to note that not all stress is bad. Wonderful things in our lives are significant sources of anxiety and tension.

When a client came to me recently complaining of feeling rundown and at a loss about how to cope with her life, I asked if any particularly stressful events were occurring. She told me, "Well, no. My daughter got married last month and I started a wonderful new job two weeks ago. But they're good things so they shouldn't be a problem." I smiled and told her that stress can arise from both positive and negative events in our lives.

Any sort of change, no matter whether we welcome it into our lives or try to push it away, puts us in a new environment that requires us to expend large amounts of energy to get reoriented. Like stress, the challenges you face in creating your personal sacred text cannot automatically be labeled bad and also should not be consistently avoided.

Challenges may not arrive as planned or be invited, but they will always be opportunities to move into the next level of growth. There may be moments when, because you are low on energy or already overwhelmed by other issues, it would be prudent to postpone or table working on your personal sacred text for a while. When I was struggling to meet deadlines on class assignments in graduate school and encountered a challenge in writing a piece of scripture at the same time, I had to learn to put away my sacred text until the school pressures had passed. To divide my energies between two challenging tasks only shortchanged efforts in both areas. But you cannot avoid challenges indefinitely. I guarantee they cannot be sent to the bottom of the river with the hope of never seeing them again. There is no boulder heavy enough to keep challenges down forever. Life is cyclical. They will resurface. You will continue to be faced with these challenges until you meet them.

~

What You
Need Before
You Start

AFTER SELECTING your destination, reviewing your itinerary, and mapping your route, you are finally at the edge of embarking on your journey. Now's the time to figure out what you need to start the process of creating your personal sacred text. You should take great care with your preparations. Carefully assembling all of the necessary elements up front will save you many hassles while you are in the middle of the creation process. Interrupting the flow may result in a temporary but frustrating derailment. My years of experience have shown me some items that are valuable to gather together ahead of time.

An Open Soul

IN ORDER TO MAXIMIZE the benefits of creating your personal sacred text, you need to recognize Spirit's presence in the places, people, and circumstances you encounter. Spirit is omnipresent. There is not a single human being, no matter how much he or she denies or engages in behavior that might indicate otherwise, who is without an indwelling higher power. Every encounter with Spirit will provide you with knowledge and wisdom that will shape your life. Consequently, one of your greatest challenges will be seeking to recognize that presence anywhere and everywhere.

Your ability to detect Spirit and his handiwork along the way will depend largely on the openness of your soul to the world. The more rigid and narrow your perceptions of how Spirit presents himself and works in the universe, the less likely you are to recognize his omnipresence. Any boundaries you define will only limit the wisdom you can gain.

To increase your encounters with Spirit, cultivate an open-soul approach to life. This requires an attitude of receptivity. Seek clues of divine presence in *every* person, place, and circumstance you encounter. Broaden your definition of what constitutes a sign that Spirit is at work to include more than those actions or words overtly connected to spirituality and religion. Anyplace there is love, compassion, wisdom, generosity, acceptance, and kindness, Spirit is present. Look beyond the negatives and seek instead to locate positive qualities. Such a focus will never fail to turn up the presence of Spirit.

Initially this may be difficult. Taking an open-soul approach is a skill, and all skills take practice to develop. For this reason, we will begin our review of resources for creating your personal sacred text with the sacred texts of the world's major religions and those with a clear spiritual undertone, such as hymns and prayers. Looking through these selections will invariably turn up the presence of Spirit and hone your ability to detect him. As we travel into more secular resources, your soul will open and your ability to identify Spirit will improve. Eventually you will be able to see him in even the most secular of settings. Some of my most delightful discoveries of great wisdom have been in such worldly places as comic strips and rock music. I cherish those pieces of my sacred text even more than those taken directly from religious literature because they symbolize my victory over my previously closed soul.

A Willingness to Explore

LIKE THE DEVELOPMENT of an open soul, it may take you some time to build up your willingness to explore new areas. Allow yourself the grace to grow by gradually moving from safe areas into more challenging ones. While doing so takes an investment of courage, it will bring you rewards that far outweigh the energy needed to step forward into the lesser-known places.

Create a support system by establishing a partnership or group with others who are undertaking the process of compiling their sacred texts. It need not be a large group with a great deal of formality; the elements of trust, openness, and encouragement are much more important than form. The group's purpose will be to help you take the difficult steps and provide a safety net if you stumble. More details about forming and running a partnership or group are available in chapter 15.

When exploring becomes particularly challenging, focus on your willingness to participate rather than on your specific actions. As a therapist I have found time and time again that cultivating an internal process eventually will lead to an external shift in behavior. As you mentally seek to remain open and willing, in time the courage to take the next step will rise from within you.

An Adventurous Spirit

A LOVE FOR ADVENTURE will serve you well on your journey. Although in our society we usually associate adventure with thrill-seeking behavior such as skydiving and bungee jumping, this is a misconception. Adventure can be found in any circumstance if only we seek it. Building a fort out of pillows and cardboard in the living room with your toddler can be just as exciting as your first ski trip, if what you are aiming to do is express your love of life's vast opportunities.

You will be able to find incredible wisdom at any time while creating your personal sacred text if you involve yourself wholly with the experience. Knowledge and discernment arise from not only an intellectual involvement with what you encounter but an emotional and spiritual involvement as well. When a friend wholeheartedly recommends a book on a topic that looks like it has nothing to offer you, don't pass it by. Stop and engage yourself with it. Seek an adventure and one will surely arise.

I have learned incredible lessons from simple circumstances and unassuming people because I took the time to pause and approach them with an attitude that expected adventure. One summer, having been camping for several weeks, I made a visit to the local laundry. A family folding clothes next to me told me of the cancer their youngest son had struggled with the previous winter. They had prayed for a miracle of healing, but just before Christmas it seemed their child's death was imminent. They prepared to let their son go at the same time they celebrated a season of birth. Days before the holiday he succumbed to an infection that usually is fatal. Yet as they waited by his bedside they witnessed a miraculous transformation. It was as if the infection were burning away the cancer rather than extinguishing his life. Within days, and in time for Christmas, he was home and in complete remission. An event as ordinary as going to the laundry yielded the most amazing of stories. I treasure this one in my personal sacred day as a testament to the power of prayer and healing.

Try this exercise. When you are sitting at stoplights, a usually mundane and adventureless moment, observe the other drivers waiting around you. What are they doing? Are children being calmed, spouses embraced, or tears being shed? What are the stories being shared and lessons to be learned? This exercise has provided me with some poignant and bittersweet glimpses into others' lives when they think no one is looking.

Life is always an adventure if we are willing to receive it. Step into each opportunity with expectancy. Take a moment and engage yourself with the person, place, or circumstance before you arrive at a decision about what it has to offer you. You will seldom be disappointed if you choose to approach rather than retreat.

A Commitment to Integrity

CREATING YOUR PERSONAL sacred text is rooted in the ideas of individuality and personal choice. In order to find the path that is best suited to you, you will need to be honest with yourself about who you are. Considering the rejection of your friends or family due to your choosing something they will not like or approve of is not a part of this process. The only person hurt by your choice to compromise on what you truly want and need will be you.

If you have had little practice being true to yourself, choose to find out who you are on your journey. As you discover bits and pieces of yourself, make a commitment to own them completely and protect them with integrity.

This will be a journey of self-awareness and discovery for you, regardless of how well you know yourself when you begin. As you travel, you may be challenged to turn away from your quest for truth. Painful circumstances may arise or people may confront you in ways that you have never considered. An encounter with something from your past may be unexpected and fearsome. Or you may consciously choose to delve into a sensitive area that you know needs to be dealt with and resolved. Your reaction to these challenges may be to take the easy road—away from the truth.

I had been working with Brandon for months on a piece of scripture he was writing about his wife's death. It was filled with beautiful language and a touching tribute to the life they had shared together. But it lacked the powerful emotions of anger and injustice that brewed just underneath the surface. When you encounter experiences like this you will be tempted, as Brandon was, to choose a safe but dishonest compromise. If you do so, you will be laying a stone in your foundation that will not support healthy growth above it. In those moments stop, access your support system, and reaffirm your commitment to finding the path of truth. Such a choice will never leave regrets for the future. When Brandon was able to include his complete experiences with the whirling aftermath of feelings following his wife's death, he finished not only his scripture but a large part of his personal healing as well.

The Writer Inside You

EVEN THOUGH this journey will include writing your own scripture, it is not necessary for you to be experienced or accomplished with a pen or keyboard. Many of us enjoyed creating poems and stories when we were children but were squelched in our desire to continue pursuing such creative pleasures by negative judgments of others. There is no judge, English teacher, or critic for your scripture. The only person you will need to please is yourself.

That writer inside you never went completely away. Even if you've never met your writer, I promise she is there, just as I know there is a divine presence within you that possesses all the creative power and ability you will ever need. One of my greatest pleasures from teaching others how to create their personal sacred text is helping people who thought they could never write their own scripture complete their first project. What joy we both felt when they discovered they could express themselves in written form!

Writing Tools

FINALLY, YOU WILL NEED tools to record your discoveries, lessons, and adventures. Paper, pens, your laptop computer, and even a library card are all good choices to consider. When purchasing paper and writing instruments, even ink cartridges for your printer, always check to make sure that they are acid and lignin free. With the growing popularity of scrapbooking, many products now clearly state whether they meet those criteria. These archival-quality materials won't fade, yellow, or deteriorate over the years.

I recommend that you begin a file folder or purchase some sort of organizer to keep all of your notes, selections, and project elements secure in one place. Although you will be assembling your final selections into the format of a sacred text, notes, photocopied possibilities, and drafts of your personal writing will need safekeeping. Having your material accessible and organized will help you stay focused and prevents the process from becoming overwhelming.

Physical and Spiritual Stamina

YOUR JOURNEY will transform your spiritual practice. You will be asked to try different methods of stretching and expanding the way you conceive of and commune with Spirit. In order to get the most from these spiritual exercises, you will need plenty of flexibility, openness, and energy.

Keep yourself at peak levels by taking care of yourself physically, eating properly, sleeping sufficiently, and exercising your body. Self-care in any area will increase your ability to maximize your creative process. Include in the creation process anything that gives you strength and allows you to work efficiently. Affirmations can give you power, relationships can provide courage, and beliefs can yield nourishment.

PART TWO

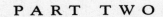

Assembling
Your Personal
Sacred Text

Truth is the fruit
of spiritual exploration . . .

— THICH NHAT HANH

FIVE

Documenting
Each Selection

SOMEWHERE, in the dark corners of several closets and drawers, I have a lifetime of photographs stuffed into large manila envelopes, shoe boxes, and even shopping bags. Some are decades old now, others are more recent, and a few date to my parents' childhood. If I died tomorrow I'm sure the unlucky person charged with cleaning out my belongings would think them trash rather than treasures.

With all of the demands on our time these days, organizing photographs seems a pretty low priority. As modern as our technology is, it cannot help us label old pictures of our grandmother's family or those snapshots of your son's championship softball team. Despite being a low priority in the grind of daily life, documenting your memories is of significant importance in the overall scheme of things. Without notations stating who is in the picture, when it was taken, and what the circumstances were, you risk losing that information forever. It is wonderful to have the photographs, but they are incomplete without the supporting documentation.

This sort of record keeping is important not just with photographs from your real-life adventures but with your spiritual journey to create a personal sacred text as well. The stories behind your selections are an integral part of each entry, not just for you but for those who may have the privilege of reading your sacred text, should you choose to share it. Consequently, each piece you add should be accompanied by several basic elements of documentation. If it is a selection authored by someone else, those details are when and where you found it; when you added it to your text; and why you chose to do so. If the piece is one you wrote, your documentation should note when you wrote it; what inspired you to write the piece; when you added it to your text; and why you chose to include it. You can place this information at the conclusion of the selection or on a facing or corresponding page.

Imagine how much more precious and meaningful your work will be to your family and friends if each excerpt is accompanied by an explanation of why you added it and what its significance was in your understanding of and relating to Spirit. Can you see how beneficial it will be to *you* to be able to review selections you made years ago, observe your evolving beliefs and thoughts, see the dynamic growth you've experienced, and marvel at the wisdom and clarification you've received? While the explanation behind the choices for including a piece of work is not the primary focus of your text, it greatly increases the power and usefulness of what you create.

The importance of documenting your selections is so great that I want to devote this entire chapter to it *before* you even begin making your journey. I want you to be familiar enough with the documentation process that it is hanging around in the back of your mind while you're making your selections. If it is, then you can be storing the information you'll need later while the process is under way. Nothing is more annoying than having to reconstruct data after the fact, especially if you didn't know you were going to need it but could have gathered it very easily if you had known.

I also want you to begin the documentation process at the same time you start making selections or writing your own scripture. Remember all those photographs stored in the shoe boxes? Somehow just seeing the sheer number of them is enough to kill the motivation to put them in albums. The task seems too overwhelming even to start, and you begin to avoid looking at the pictures because they remind you that you have a lot of work left undone. Yet had that part of the process been integrated into the picture-taking activities as a natural follow-up to receiving the developed photographs, the end result would have been an enjoyable and accessible family heirloom rather than the next generation's headache.

You don't have to add the item to your text immediately upon finding it, but do note the details you will need for your documentation as soon as you decide to include a piece. Sometimes I will find something and it so abruptly catches my attention that I rush to include it in my text along with the corresponding story. At other times I'll find something and know I want it to be a part of my book, but the time and opportunity are simply not there. In those instances I make or take a hard copy of it in any way I can, jot some notes on it about why I like it and where I found it, then tuck it into my text for formal inclusion at a later date. I've been known to rip articles from magazines, photocopy passages from books, print parts of a Web page, and even write down a quote on a napkin. Sometimes these entries remain crammed into the back of my text for months before I can recopy them. That's okay. Just be sure to make a few notes about these entries you want to document so that you are not racking your brain months later to remember the details. Otherwise, your hard-won entries will go the way of the photos in the shoe-box scenario.

Documentation for Selections
from Others' Material

WHEN THE PIECE you are adding to your text was authored by someone else, it is important to give him or her appropriate credit by noting the source of the selection. Also include why you found the piece meaningful and decided to add it to your text. Here's a sample from my personal sacred text.

PRAYER OF ST. PATRICK

Christ be with me, Christ before me, Christ behind me,
Christ in me, Christ beneath me, Christ above me,
Christ on my right, Christ on my left.
Christ where I live, Christ where I sit, Christ where I arise,
Christ in the heart of every one who thinks of me,
Christ in the mouth of every one who speaks of me,
Christ in every eye that sees me,
Christ in every ear that hears me.

Date added to my text: September 30, 1997
Where and when found: First heard during a sermon in 1996. In September 1997 I rediscovered it in *Prayer: Language of the Soul*
Why significant: At times I have felt so alone I feared my heart would break from the grief of loneliness. In other moments, when all of the past betrayals crowd to the front of my mind, I struggle to feel safe in this world. When I heard Michael recite this prayer I knew Spirit was giving me a tool to combat those feelings of isolation and vulnerability.

Why added: I chose this piece because it brings me comfort. The message and the manner in which it is presented appeal to me. It also echoes the Native American Prayer to the Seven Directions that I love so much.

DATE YOU ADDED OR INTENDED TO ADD THE SELECTION TO YOUR TEXT

SOMETIMES YOU WILL decide to include a piece in your text before you get the chance actually to make the addition. Probably you will find it more helpful to track your intention rather than the corresponding action. We all get busy and the things we wanted to get done end up delayed no matter how determined we are. Creating a sacred text is kind of like painting a picture. Each brushstroke adds a needed element, and gradually you begin to see the complete image emerge. In order to gain the benefit of watching your spiritual development unfold, focus the date you add a selection to your text on your intention rather than the outward action. The picture will come together based on your intentions.

WHERE AND WHEN YOU FOUND THE PIECE

THIS ONE IS PRETTY self-explanatory. Note the name of the work you took the piece from, the date you first read it, and under what circumstances you encountered it. The date for this portion of the documentation may be very different from the one you noted under the prior heading. I first heard the Prayer of St. Patrick in 1996, during a sermon at church. The next year I found it again in a book on prayer and found it so compelling that I decided to add it to my text immediately. I first read Ella Wheeler Wilcox's poem "As If by Fire" in 1983, when I had to memorize it for an American Literature class. In 1994 when I was making my initial entries into my sacred text it was one of the first pieces I added.

As If by Fire
by Ella Wheeler Wilcox (1850–1919)

Sometimes I feel so passionate a yearning
For spiritual perfection here below
This vigorous frame with healthful fervor burning
Seems my determined foe

So actively it makes a stern resistance
So cruelly sometimes it wages war
Against a wholly spiritual existence
Which I am striving for

It interrupts my soul's intense devotions
Some hope it strangles of divinist birth
With a swift rush of violent emotions
Which links me to the earth

It is as if two mortal foes contended
Within my bosom in a deadly strife
One for the loftier aims for souls intended
One for this earthly life

And yet I know this very war within me
Which brings out all my willpower and control
This very conflict at the last shall win me
The loved and longed for goal

The very fire which seems sometimes so cruel
Is white light, that shows me my own strength
A furnace, fed by divinist fuel
It may become at length

Ah! when in the immortal ranks enlisted
I sometimes wonder if we shall not find
That not by deeds, but by what we've resisted
Our places will be assigned

Date added to my text: July 1, 1994
Where & when found: Anthology of American Poetry, 1983, during American Literature class.
Why significant: I loved this poem from the moment I found it more than a decade ago. It was the first one I memorized for class because I thought it captured my own internal turmoil so well. I love the last two lines the most!
Why added: Succinctly put, it has haunted me for years. From time to time it comes to mind and I can hear my own voice reciting it for class. It seems bonded to my soul and demands inclusion.

Perhaps you will hear a song one day while listening to the radio on your way to work, but it won't be until you read the lyrics that accompany the compact disc months later that you decide to add the song to your text. On the other hand, you may read a column in the local paper today that speaks to you so strongly you immediately decide to include it. The circumstances are all part of that larger puzzle you are constructing. You may hear or see something that is meaningful but not especially significant in the moment but years later a circumstance or life lesson brings it to your memory again. All of a sudden it has a tremendous amount of wisdom that you didn't see earlier. These are all-important elements of the underlying story of your text's creation.

WHY THIS PIECE IS SIGNIFICANT

IN A FEW SENTENCES note why this selection is meaningful to you. Why did it grab your attention? What part of your life does it address? Is there a particular message it conveys to you? How does it capture your own story? We are all unique creatures and, consequently, how we interpret a work will be different from how the readers of our text might. Don't leave them guessing. Explain why and how this particular selection touched you.

In this section of my documentation I focus on specific details and facts. I'll note what was going on in my life that made this piece so special. It's not unusual for me to say something like "I found this when I felt overwhelmed by what was happening with Adam. It captured what I felt better than I ever could with my own words." If a couple of lines in particular grabbed me, I'll point them out and explain why.

WHY YOU ADDED THIS PIECE TO YOUR TEXT

UNDOUBTEDLY you will find many selections that are meaningful to you at one moment or another in your life. But only a small percentage of those will be significantly representative of your spiritual beliefs and development that they will warrant inclusion in your sacred text. We will discuss the sorting and selection criteria in depth in chapter 10. But for now, the shoe box of old photos is a terrific example to illustrate my point. If you could create only one album of the most meaningful pictures in your life, you would have to be pretty exclusive in your choice. Many photographs will be special, but only a few will have such weight and importance that they merit inclusion in your sole photo album. The dividing line probably will be between those photos that have a singular or momentary significance and those that have multiple meanings or represent a whole era in your life, a transformative moment, or an important turning point.

Your explanation in this portion of your sacred text probably will focus more on your thoughts, feelings, and beliefs than concrete fact. Note why, of all the pieces in the world that had personal meaning, you chose this particular one. What made this selection so vital that it had to be included? Does it address a recurring issue or pattern in your life? Does it capture a particular piece of wisdom that now makes up a core concept about your understanding of and relationship with Spirit?

Documentation for
Your Own Scripture Writing

WHEN INCLUDING details about selections that you authored, the focus shifts from noting the source of the work to the source of the inspiration for the piece. You will still note dates and why you included the work in your text, but now you will add the motivation behind your writing it.

To Behold Peniel
by Bobbi L. Parish
("Peniel" is the Hebrew word for "face of God")

I was born into the world on bended knee, head bowed low.
Fresh of heart, but already filled with the sin of my forefathers.
I sought forgiveness from the god of my family.
Runt of the litter, my search was crowded out.
Priests, nuns, and pious laity nursed at the breast of blessing, I
    starved in solitude.

"Why doesn't the mother love me?"
"You're too selfish," the plump ones cried, stomping circles for their
    naps.
"Make yourself lower."
"Destroy yourself so she can remake you in her image."
"Her will, not yours."

From knees to belly, face pressed into the dirt,
I pulled weeds of selfness from my being.
Tilling the soil with submission and brokenness, waiting to be found
    worthy,
To be filled with the mother's love.

A flower grew so firm and fast I could not pull it from the earth.
Bitter tears of final hopelessness strengthened its resolve.
"Why do you weep?" a kindly gardener asked.
"It keeps me from the mother's love."
"No, no," he sighed. "It is your mother's love.
Let the garden grow lush and full.
Its beauty was destined at your birth,
When love and worth exchanged forever."

My hand in his he pulled me tall,
Face to face, eye to eye.
His breath still sweeps across my cheek.

Date(s) written: March 3–5, 1998. *Date added to my text:*
   March 8, 1998

Why written: Listening to Rev. Robinson relate Jacob's physical struggle with God stirred my soul. That was me! I had
   been wrestling with God for years: Who are you? Why do
   you allow me to suffer? Why won't you bless me!? And yet
   those difficult times were the catalyst for the revisioning of
   my image of God. In the end I received an enormous blessing of being able to stand upright and behold God face-to-
   face.

Why added: I have tried before to capture my struggles to reim-
   age God in words. I was never happy with the result. This
   time, with the Peniel image in hand, it virtually "wrote itself." I love the imagery and the style of the piece. It conveys what I feel perfectly.

DATE WRITTEN

YOU PROBABLY WILL find it most helpful to make this the date
you completed the final form of the piece. I tend to write and rewrite
pieces over the course of several months. In this section I note the date

when I decided it had reached finished form. There will be more signifi-cance attached to the finished product than the initial drafts, so this is the date you should choose. If it seems particularly significant to note when you started it or over what period of time you worked on it, that's fine to note too.

DATE ADDED TO YOUR TEXT

THIS FIELD HAS the same purpose and meaning of the one noted previously. If I finish a piece in December, decide to add it to my text in January, but don't actually get around to it until March, I will note the January date in this field.

WHY YOU WROTE THIS PIECE

THIS NOTATION is similar to the "Why this piece is significant" sec-tion discussed earlier. Again, focus on the circumstances under which you wrote the piece. What motivated you to write it? What were you trying to articulate or capture with your words? Was there a purpose or motive behind writing this piece? Did you write it solely for yourself, or was there an intended audience? Did you write it as part of a class as-signment, journal entry, or as the result of wisdom or insight received during a period of reflection or meditation? All of these are facts to note briefly.

WHY YOU ADDED THIS PIECE TO YOUR TEXT

THIS NOTATION is identical to the one in the prior section.

IT IS NOT NECESSARY to make your comments in any of these sec-tions for documentation lengthy or comprehensive. The goal is to cap-ture the main points that support the story behind the corresponding selection. If you demand yourself to wax eloquent, you probably will end up avoiding the task because it takes too much effort. One or two sentences are fine. Complete sentences are not even required. If bulleted points are quicker and easier for you to make, then please use them, but don't write anything so cryptic that readers will not be able to understand your notes without you sitting there to translate. Keep it simple but functional.

Not all of these items may work for you. Experiment with them as it feels appropriate. Please, though, eliminate a category of notation only if it does not seem applicable, not because it seems like too much work. If there are additional items you think you need to add to a particular piece or the entire process, do not hesitate to include those. This is, after all, your *personal* sacred text.

Six

Assembling
Your Selections
into a Text Format

ARE YOU ONE of the millions of people worldwide who write in a journal? Keeping notes on our life's activities for the purpose of record keeping, expression, and reflection is an increasingly popular trend. Perhaps you use a daily planner rather than a diary. Both, in my opinion, are forms of keeping records of the events in our lives. If you don't currently practice journaling in one form or another, I'm sure that you are at least familiar with the concept of jotting down your thoughts and feelings in some format.

While the overarching concept seems to be universal, the variety of journal styles is too numerous to count. What you choose to write in and how you accomplish that task can vary sharply from the way your neighbor or friend keeps a journal. Some people use simple bound blank books and others, elaborate multisectioned binders. Most make entries in their journals in chronological order, but some sort their entries by type. You make decisions on how you will journal based on your personal preferences and individual purpose for keeping records. Each choice alters the process and product to some degree. But that's part of the attractiveness of journaling—it can be changed to suit your unique situation.

Your personal sacred text shares many of the qualities and characteristics of a journal. It is, in essence, the record of your spiritual journey. You can keep and assemble your text in a variety of ways. With the freedom to alter any number of these features, you can customize this record to meet your individual purpose and personality without affecting the overall purpose of creating a personal sacred text. This chapter will provide you with several different options and help you choose among them.

Like learning how to document each selection, you need to decide how you will assemble your text before you begin your journey. Knowing how you will create your text allows you to begin the process immediately upon making your first selection. If you're still trying to decide about this after you start, you run the risk of collecting your selections in a temporary holding space, such as a file folder. Like the shoe box full of photographs, your folder will soon fill up with material and the task of organizing it will seem so overwhelming, it will turn you off the entire process.

Additionally, if you begin your text in a haphazard manner, it's difficult to use and review it as you go along. Those patterns and developments you would be able to see if your selections were growing in an ordered manner will be buried under the disorder. You will cheat yourself out of the some of the rich rewards of creating a personal sacred text every moment that it isn't easily readable and accessible.

There are two basic elements of assembling your text: format and order.

Format

IN THE CONTEXT of creating a personal sacred text, I define format as the type and style of medium in which you choose to record your selections. For example, you could write your passages out in long-hand on ordinary notebook paper or you may choose to keep your entries on computer disk. Myriad available options are too numerous to itemize, but I have assembled a list of those that have proven to be the easiest for me to use over the course of the last decade.

A SPIRAL-BOUND NOTEBOOK

YOU CAN'T DENY the ease of obtaining, transporting, and affording this method of recording your personal sacred text. A drawback is that it's impossible to reorder the pages or add pages to it later on. You may end up with several notebooks, which cancels out the portability benefit and also diminishes the opportunities to reorganize your text once you record an entry. It's also not the most aesthetically pleasing or durable method available. If you choose this option, use the type of acid-free pens and paper discussed in chapter 4.

A THREE-RING BINDER

THIS METHOD IS also readily available and affordable. It isn't as compact as a spiral-bound notebook, but it is much more durable. You can rearrange or add pages as necessary, organizing them with dividers and even including page protectors and pockets if that suits your taste. This method also allows you the freedom of writing out your selection longhand or printing it off your word processor. While you can purchase binders that allow you to insert customized covers, which is a huge plus over the notebook, a clunky binder may still not have the aesthetic qualities some think a sacred text deserves.

BOUND JOURNAL/BLANK BOOKS

THESE VOLUMES can be found in almost every drug, department, and bookstore. They are much more attractive than binders or spiral-bound notebooks, but they have many of the drawbacks associated with the latter. You can't add or reorder pages, and unless you want to paste computer-generated selections into it, you're stuck creating your text in longhand. Another drawback is that over the years, you may be faced with a sacred text consisting of several volumes. But as these books are generally smaller than letter-size notebooks, they will be easier to transport. They are also more durable than notebooks, but not as long lasting as binders.

COMPUTER DISK

IN THIS ERA of technological wizardry, keeping your personal sacred text on disk, whether on a floppy, hard drive, CD-ROM, or Zip drive, may be the option that most suits your lifestyle. Of course, you'll need either a printed hard copy, which kicks you into all the drawbacks and advantages of the various paper options I've discussed, or a laptop to have your text readily available to you. If you choose to store your text on disk, *back it up frequently*. I have worked with more than one author who's experienced the agony of losing years of work after a disk was lost or damaged and data could not be recovered. Also, be sure to keep your technology current. It will do you no good to keep your files stored on three-and-a-half-inch floppy disks if they become obsolete a few years down the road. If you are especially gifted in website design, you may wish to place portions of your text online. Sharing it in this manner with your friends and family may be a powerful method of declaring your thoughts and ideas about Spirit.

ARCHIVAL-QUALITY SCRAPBOOKS

THE LAST TEN years have seen an explosion in popularity of acid-free photo albums and scrapbooks. The beauty of this method is that you can completely customize your text. Pages can be reordered and added as needed, and you can make your text as elaborate as you like with all the acid-free markers, stickers, and paper on the market. Expense and portability can be problematic, though. Albums can cost upward of $50, and that doesn't include any embellishments, such as stickers or special papers, you may wish to have. Most scrapbooks are quite large, up to 15 × 17 inches, so they can be quite cumbersome. Despite these disadvantages, this is the method I have chosen to create my personal sacred text. I purchased a smaller album, 10 × 10 inches, and have spent a great deal of time customizing it. As a very visually oriented person, aesthetics are important to me. This method has allowed me to create a text that reflects the sacred nature of all it embodies to me.

Acid-free scrapbooking supplies are more readily available than ever. You should be able to find albums, papers, and embellishments at your local craft supply store, and a number of books and online resources can help you with the process. See these resources for more information:

Making Scrapbooks: A Complete Guide to Preserving Your Treasured Memories by Vanessa-Ann
This is one of the most complete references on acid-free archival scrapbooking on the market.

Cut 'n Fun: http://www.cutnfun.com
This site has an excellent online catalog listing acid-free albums, paper, pens, and printer inks as well as instructions on scrapbooking and links to other resources.

Scrap Happy: http://www.telepath.com/bcarson/scrap_happy
Scrap Happy provides extensive links along with online catalog and informational resources for scrapbooking supplies.

HANDMADE BOOKS

IF A CUSTOM-MADE TEXT is really what you're after, there is no substitute for making your own paper and then binding it by hand. While this requires a lot of time and effort, it results in a priceless and valuable product that you and your family will cherish for years to come. To cut down on the required investment of energy, you can always purchase the paper and only bind the pages yourself. Papermaking and binding supplies, like scrapbooking materials, have been more readily available over the last few years. But you will still need some assistance for purchasing and completing the process. See these resources for more help:

The Art and Craft of Papermaking: Step-by-Step Instructions for Creating Distinctive Handmade Paper by Sophie Dawson
This is a concise, simple guide to papermaking. It is a great resource for the beginner.

The Art of the Handmade Book: Designing, Decorating, and Binding One-of-a-Kind Books by Flora Fennimore
Fennimore has written a comprehensive book that details every aspect of the bookmaking process.

Cover to Cover by Shereen LaPlantz
Another good guide to handcrafting books. It includes a lot of information on embellishments and design.

Making Your Own Paper by Marianne Saddington
Saddington has written an excellent introduction to the art of papermaking. This book should be in the library of anyone interested in the topic.

Take some time to think about each of these format options before you make your selection. Consider your personal preferences and needs, such as how much time and money you can invest. The importance of appearance, durability, and portability are also points to consider. If you have experience keeping a journal or daily planner, this is probably the most comparable factor to examine in making your decision. Do a little bit of shopping at your local craft or stationery store. I'm not suggesting you spend hours obsessing over the method you choose, but I do recommend that your decision be careful and deliberate. Format is part of the individualized and unique aspect of creating a personal sacred text. Whatever you choose should reflect who you are and be easily integrated into your life.

Order

THIS IS THE SECOND element of text assembly that you need to consider prior to beginning your creation process. While most of us have been exposed only to the chronological method of compiling a journal, you can consider two other options in the creation of your personal sacred text. All three have been used with great success in the major sacred texts of the world's religions. Each will give your work a different flavor without altering your underlying process. Your choice in this area, as with your format selection, has more to do with personal preference than functionality. So don't be afraid to try something other than what you're used to if it seems to suit your lifestyle and taste.

CHRONOLOGICAL

THIS IS PROBABLY the choice that you are most familiar with because our lives tend to be organized around time and schedule. It is also the simplest way to assemble your text because it requires only that you record each selection in the order that you found or wrote it. There are two major benefits of using this technique. The first is that it is so familiar and therefore requires little orientation. The second is that it is the best one to easily demonstrate the dynamic process of your spiritual development. If you record your selections in this way, a quick review will reveal how your beliefs and ideas have evolved over time. This is a powerful element of a personal sacred text for you and your reader. Choose this method if you want to maximize the benefits of charting your spiritual growth.

BY GENRE

IN THIS METHOD you will group the selections in your sacred text according to the type of writing or artwork. For example, you would place all of your poems in one section, your photos or artwork in another, and your stories in another. The benefit of using this order is that you can easily access materials that suit your specific reading/studying needs. The downside is that it takes more time to assemble than a simple chronological order and it's harder to see a progression in your development. This is the way I have chosen to order my sacred text because I found myself continually making choices about what I wanted to review based on genre. Sometimes I'm just more in the mood for poetry than an essay. Or I need a quick proverb to carry through the day. Organizing my text into subsections titled poetry, prose, and proverbs has made it very functional and accessible. And accessibility is, after all, the primary reason to customize your work.

BY SUBJECT

THIS IS A POPULAR method of ordering with which you probably have a lot of experience. Subject or thematic categorization dominates any sort of research, from the World Wide Web to mail-order shopping. Perhaps you would like to have sections dealing with specific periods in your life, such as childhood memories or your experiences as a parent. Maybe you will choose to divide your sacred text according to lessons about abstract concepts such as grace, love, and healing. Have particular themes repeated themselves in your life? They might make logical sections. For me topics such as loss and grief, triumph over difficulty, and turning points would be natural categories to explore. Like the genre ordering, sorting your personal sacred text by subject takes more time and does not show your spiritual development as easily as the chronological method, but its simplicity is very attractive.

.   .   .

OF COURSE, you may combine these three methods into a customized order. For example, if you choose a subject grouping, you can always order the selections chronologically within the subsection. Or if you divide them by genre, you can order them further by subject.

WHILE VARIOUS CHOICES among these format and order options may be appropriate or inappropriate for your individual needs, it's important to note that none is wrong or right. All are simply different. Selecting one method over another will not significantly alter either the process or the outcome of creating a personal sacred text. The purpose of the methods is to help you customize your personal sacred text in a way that is the most comfortable and, consequently, fruitful for you. Feel free to experiment until you find the method that suits you best. Keep in mind, though, that switching from one format or order to another may be a lot of work. This doesn't mean you shouldn't make a change if it seems wise, just that you'll need to stop for a while and reorient yourself.

PART THREE

~

Making Selections from Existing Material

And when you shall receive these things, I would exhort you that you would ask God, the Eternal Father, in the name of Christ, if these things are not true; and if you ask with a sincere heart, with a real intent, having faith in Christ, he will manifest the truth of it to you, by the power of the Holy Ghost.

— THE BOOK OF MORMON,
MORONI 10:4

~

SEVEN

Major
Sacred Texts

FOR SOME OF YOU, this may be your first introduction to the sacred texts of the major world religions, or even to the religions themselves. Don't worry, there is no prerequisite course work needed. The information provided here will be very introductory and focused on the texts rather than a recitation of the history and beliefs of each religion.

However, if you are seeking a beginning resource before diving into this chapter, I recommend *How Do You Spell God?: Answers to the Big Questions From Around the World* by Rabbi Marc Gellman and Monsignor Thomas Hartman. It provides an excellent introduction to world religion. Yes, it is written for children of about middle and junior high school age. But its simple, jargon-free language makes it a basic primer for individuals of any age. It addresses a wide range of topics, from "What question does each religion want to answer most?" to "When are the Holy Days?" My favorite thing about this book is that it does not section each religion into a separate chapter, which can make comparing and seeking common threads difficult. Instead, Gellman and Hartman answer the same question for each tradition under every topic heading. For our purposes, this is a wonderful arrangement.

I also recommend Huston Smith's *Illustrated World's Religions: A Guide to Our Wisdom Tradition.* The exquisite photographs in this book will take your breath. Pair it with Smith's eloquent prose summarizing each religion's history and beliefs and you can understand why this book has been in print since 1958. For all of you visually oriented people, this volume is a must.

If you want a little more than the basic introduction offered in *How Do You Spell God?* Steven S. Sadleir has written a useful volume: *The Spiritual Seeker's Guide: The Complete Source for Religions and Spiritual Groups of the World.* From Buddhism to Rastafarianism, Sadleir provides a two-to-three–page synopsis of the history and beliefs of each group as well as recommendations for further reading.

Because the process of creating a personal sacred text is truly a mystical journey, you may wish to read an introduction to the world's religions from that specific vantage point. *Mysticism: Holiness East and West* by Denise Lardner Carmody and John Tully Carmody traces the history of the mystical movements within each of the major world religions. If you are, like me, a heart-centered person who relates to life through emotional experience, this book is a perfect selection.

Alternately, if you are familiar with the major sacred texts already, you may not need the resources covered in this chapter. That's okay. Skip what you know and scan the rest. In the interest of future reference I have arranged the religious traditions in alphabetical order. Each section begins with a brief synopsis of the tradition itself, and then a short history and summary is given for each major sacred text. I provide recommendations for the most accurate and readable translations, if they exist. I list translations or texts geared toward beginning students first, if available, followed by more complex and challenging selections. The individual listings conclude with any other pertinent resources. I selected books for inclusion in this chapter by asking three questions:

1. Is it typically classified by the experts as a sacred text?
2. Is there a readable translation available in English?
3. Is it compatible with the purpose of creating a personal sacred text?

Note: A great deal of spiritually oriented material may be recognized within a particular tradition as sacred but not seen as such by the world as a whole. This is particularly true of legends from shamanistic and goddess-oriented traditions. So if what you're looking for isn't here, check the listings of other spiritual resources beginning on page 98.

Buddhism

DHAMMAPADA

THIS SACRED TEXT is a collection of sayings attributed to Buddha. They survived in oral form for several centuries until 240 B.C., when they were recorded by the Council of Ashoka. The root word *Dhamma* means "moral path of life," lending to the full title's translation of "statements of principle."

The original work contains 423 aphorisms divided into 26 topical chapters. Its message centers on the importance of self-development and building strength of character as methods to reaching the ultimate goal of enlightenment. For applicability to our modern life and ease of understanding, the Dhammapada is the best primer regarding Buddha's teachings.

Thomas Cleary's translation, *The Dhammapada*, is the best available. He worked directly from the original Pali text, creating a work that is both accurate and readable. Throughout the text Cleary provides ample commentary that explains the meaning and/or context of a particular verse. He also provides cross-references to sacred literature with similar messages.

Thomas Cleary is an extremely gifted linguist and scholar of sacred literature. He is recognized as one of the foremost translators in the field. You'll see that I recommend his work on the Confucian I Ching as well as the Islamic Qur'an.

TRIPITAKA (ALSO KNOWN AS TIPITAKA)

THE TRIPITAKA is composed of three distinct parts (thus the title's translation "The Three Baskets"): the Sutra Pitka; the Vinaya Pitka; and the Abhidharma. The Sutra Pitka ("Basket of Writings") contains four or five sections, depending on the translation, detailing the life and teachings of Buddha. The Dhammapada is one small portion of this segment.

The Vinaya Pitka, "Basket of Discipline," provides detailed descriptions of the rules governing the lives of Buddhist monks and nuns. Those of you familiar with the Old Testament will find this portion to read a lot like the books of Leviticus and Numbers. It is not light reading.

The final segment, the Abhidharma ("Special Teachings"), contains the earliest teachings of Buddha. Its seven separate books focus primarily on aspects of psychology and philosophy.

Versions of the Tripitaka were recorded in Pali, Sanskrit, and Chinese. Not surprisingly, this has resulted in varying translations. Some of the differences are significant. This problem, combined with the esoteric nature of the subject matter, makes this text difficult to understand for the average layman. The only portion I recommend for beginners is *The Dhammapada* (see above). However, if you have a more advanced understanding of Buddhism and would like to read more, the best comprehensive translation I have found is *Dialogues of the Buddha* by T. W. Rhys-Davids and Caroline Rhys-Davids.

DIAMOND SUTRA AND HEART SUTRA

THERE ARE MORE than fifty sutras (Sanskrit for "thread") in the Buddhist tradition. They are typically written in a poetic format, ranging from 300 to 1,000 verses. Most are inappropriate for our purposes, because they require an in-depth knowledge of Buddhist theology to understand, and some are not even translated into English.

The two that are best known in the West and also suitable for our use are the Diamond and Heart Sutras. Both are part of the Prajnaparamita, "Supreme Essence" or "Great Transcendental Wisdom," Sutra, which is actually a collection of forty individual sutras. The Diamond Sutra was the first book ever printed; this took place in China in the year 868 B.C. Its purpose is to lead the reader into enlightenment through the central Buddhist teaching that all we perceive to be reality is actually only a projection of the mind.

The Heart Sutra, so named because it is believed to encapsulate the central teaching of the entire Prajnaparamita Sutra, is the shortest offspring of its mammoth parent. It is said to be the record of discussions between Buddha and his followers. The Heart Sutra focuses on teachings about emptiness.

For those of you struggling to transcend and have a positive outlook in spite of difficult circumstances, these two pieces of sacred literature are good choices to explore. You can find a reasonably good translation available by Edward Conze in *Buddhist Wisdom Books, Containing the Diamond Sutra and the Heart Sutra.* If there is a Buddhist community near you, you may wish to contact it to see if these pieces are recited at any time.

ZEN KOANS

KOANS ARE THE Zen Buddhist equivalent of biblical parables. They are stories used by Zen masters to instruct disciples, test their perception and insight, and help focus their attention on important principles. They focus primarily on compassion and wisdom. Although koans initially appear simple, there is a depth of meaning available to the receptive and skilled reader. Given their thought-provoking density, koans are a powerful tool for helping liberate the mind from narrow and limited thinking.

There are seven major Chinese collections of koans. The Wumenguan koans are the most popular in the West. They are said to have been transcribed by a Chinese Zen master by the name of Wumen in approximately A.D. 1183 to 1260. The collection title means "Wumen's Border Pass," which refers to the process of passing through the gate of knowledge into an understanding of the koans' meaning.

Thomas Cleary has completed the best English translation of the Wumenguan koans in his volume *Unlocking the Zen Koan*. He has done an excellent job of capturing both the poetic style and content of the original language. He enhances the collection by including commentary on each koan from a variety of other great Zen masters.

IF, UPON REVIEWING these summaries of Buddhist texts you feel overwhelmed and are thinking of avoiding them altogether, don't. First seek out *Teachings of the Buddha*. This is a compact volume of selected excerpts from the extensive library of Buddhist literature edited by Jack Kornfield, one of the most respected experts on Buddhism in the United States. After using *Teachings of the Buddha* as a guide for my initial foray, I was soon hooked and began delving into more complex literature, such as Zen koans.

Christianity

THE BIBLE

THE MAIN SACRED TEXT for Christians is the Holy Bible. Written over the course of thousands of years, from approximately 1000 B.C. to A.D. 150, it is comprised of two sections: the Old Testament and the New Testament. The Old Testament, written in Hebrew, has thirty-nine separate books attributed to a variety of authors. This portion of the Bible is mostly historical in nature, beginning with a description of the creation of the known world and concluding with the prophecy of Malachi in 430 B.C. It also contains extended listings of regulations that large segments of Christian and Jewish communities still follow.

The New Testament consists of twenty-seven books originally written in Hebrew and Aramaic. The first four books, commonly referred to as the Gospels, are parallel stories of the life and teachings of Jesus Christ. The fifth, the Acts of the Apostles, chronicles the lives of Jesus' disciples for the thirty-five years immediately following his death. The remaining books are letters written by various authors to educate, admonish, and guide the growing Christian community. This section of the Bible was written approximately 100 to 150 years after the death of Jesus Christ.

There are numerous English translations of the Bible, ranging from the traditional King James to the more contemporary New American Standard. If you are just beginning to delve into this sacred text, I suggest you read Eugene Peterson's translation, *The Message*. While not the most accurate of the versions available, it isn't intended to be. Instead, it was written in contemporary language to be easily understandable by the layperson. I absolutely love it.

For commentary on history, interpretation, and context, I recommend the *Life Application Bible*. It is a complete reference, with time lines, chapter outlines, and an extensive index, which can be particularly helpful if you're looking for passages on a specific topic.

Looking for the most historically accurate interpretation of the four Gospels? Check out the Scholar's Version published as *The Five Gospels: The Search for the Authentic Words of Jesus*. The Jesus Seminar, a panel of twenty-two nationally recognized biblical scholars, created this translation over the course of six years. They had two goals in developing this new version. First, they sought to provide the layperson with an experience similar to those who heard these stories hundreds of years ago, before they were recorded in written form. They restored the flowing, almost lyrical nature of the text and replaced outdated colloquialisms with contemporary language. Second, they wanted to produce a version with ruthless historical integrity. It was this goal that led them to include the Gospel of Thomas, a manuscript found among the

Nag Hammadi Scriptures in Egypt in 1945. The panel sorted through thousands of documents in order to determine what could be verified with certainty as the actual words of Jesus and what was more likely falsely attributed to him by the authors of the Gospels and subsequent scholars.

To make these determinations, they voted on each verse using colored beads: red for "undoubtedly"; pink for "probably"; gray for "not the words but maybe the idea undergirding them"; and black for "not at all." The Scholar's Version was then printed using the same color-coding. The percentage of red text is shockingly small! A quick visual scan reveals that Christ said very little of what we have been attributing to him for the past two thousand years.

The findings of the Jesus Seminar have been extremely controversial within the Christian community. Many denominations believe the Bible is the infallible and wholly inspired word of God. They tend to dismiss the Scholar's Version as bordering on heresy. Others nod their heads and say, "I suspected as much." For those interested in biblical history, *The Five Gospels* is worth reading for the introductory comments alone. It contains page after page of fascinating information that even I, a seminary graduate, did not know.

NAG HAMMADI SCRIPTURES

DISCOVERED AT Nag Hammadi, an Egyptian town along the Nile, in 1945, this collection of sacred literature is often referred to as the Gnostic Gospel. It is composed of fifty-three documents written on papyrus and divided into thirteen leather-bound volumes. Believed to have been written in the fourth century after Christ's death, the Nag Hammadi Scriptures include the Gospel of Truth, the Gospel According to Thomas, the Gospel of Phillip, and the Gospel According to Mary Magdalene.

If you are seeking additional information about how Jesus' followers interpreted and lived out his teachings after his death, the Nag Hammadi Scriptures are an excellent resource. In some instances, particularly on the role of women in the church, they directly contradict the writings of the Gospels and letters from the New Testament. For the best translation with an informative commentary, see *The Nag Hammadi Library* edited by James M. Robinson.

THE DEAD SEA SCROLLS

TWO YEARS AFTER the recovery of the Nag Hammadi Scriptures, the first of the Dead Sea Scrolls were unearthed in the caves at Qumran, Egypt. Nine years elapsed between the initial and final discoveries of the complete collection, which dates between 150 B.C. and A.D. 68. It includes hymns, philosophical essays, descriptions of life in the local Essene community (a sect of dissident Jews), and portions of the Old Testament.

Sections of these texts are as controversial as the Nag Hammadi Scriptures, for they too often contradict the writings of the gospels and the letters of the New Testament. If you liked the Nag Hammadi Scriptures, you will enjoy the Dead Sea Scrolls. Unfortunately, the complete text of the scrolls has not yet been fully translated. But for a good initial version, look at *The Dead Sea Scrolls in English*, edited and translated by G. Vernes.

BOOK OF MORMON

ALTHOUGH NOT WIDELY studied by all Christians, the Book of Mormon is central to the Church of Jesus Christ of Latter-day Saints. This sacred text was revealed on golden tablets to Joseph Smith in 1827 in Palmyra, New York. He believed them to have been written by the prophet Mormon about Christ's appearance in the New World following his resurrection and ascension. After translating the tablets, hidden for more than a thousand years at Palmyra, Smith published the first edition of the Book of Mormon in 1830.

The Book of Mormon has fifteen sections, or books, and covers roughly between 600 B.C. and A.D. 421. It is largely historical in nature, reading much like the Old Testament. Unlike the Bible, there is only one translation of the Book of Mormon. If you have never read it, I encourage you to at least review a copy. One of my favorite selections in my personal sacred text is about seeking and finding the truth; it is quoted on page 73.

Confucianism

I CHING

THE I CHING, "Book of Change," was originally developed as a divination manual. It consisted of sixty-four pictorial hexagrams with an accompanying text that described how to use the drawings to consult the gods. Over time it transformed into a book of wisdom focused primarily on the concept of change and decision making. By using the hexagrams and their explanatory text, the reader is guided toward the right decision that will lead to success and good fortune, avoiding mistakes, failure, and misfortune. The I Ching is as widely read in China as the Bible is in the United States.

The history of the I Ching is without solid documentation. Some scholars say the hexagrams and methods for using them were developed by three Chinese individuals: King Wen of Zhou (who reigned some time around 1100 B.C.), the Duke of Zhou (who died in 1032 B.C.), and Confucius (who lived from 551 to 479 B.C.). Others believe that the I Ching was assembled as a sacred text as early as the ninth century B.C. This date would exclude the involvement of Confucius and leave authorship in the hands of only King Wen and Duke Zhou. The I Ching became connected to Confucius, they argue, only when his followers rewrote it and superimposed his teachings onto the hexagram divination process.

The controversy does not detract from the value of the I Ching. Whoever wrote it crafted a timeless text about the process of change.

My favorite translation is Edward L. Shaughnessey's *I Ching: The Classic of Changes*, because it is both readable and accurate, based on the newly discovered Mawangdui manuscript.

The best description of how to use the I Ching hexagrams is in Sarah Dening's *Everyday I Ching*. A Jungian analyst, Dening provides an easy-to-use guidebook for applying this ancient method to contemporary problems.

If you are looking for books with illustrations, try R. L. Wing's *Illustrated I Ching*. Although the translation is not as good as Shaughnessey's, the beautiful Chinese artwork more than compensates. If you're visually oriented and like the message of the I Ching, you will want to add this book to your library. When you move into writing your own scripture, the images will serve as a rich source of inspiration.

For a complete visual experience, try several of the online I Ching programs on the Internet. The best one I have found is at http://www.iching.com. It walks you through the simple process of asking the I Ching oracle a question, then casting stones into a reflecting pool. Their landing points provide the program with the information needed to determine which hexagram applies to your current situation. Finally, it gives the pictorial representation of that sign and the corresponding written interpretation.

CONFUCIAN CANON

RECORDED IN THE LATE twelfth century A.D. by Chinese scholar Chu Hsi, the Confucian Canon consists of Five Classics and Four Books. They contain a collection of sayings attributed to Confucius collected by his pupils in the seventy years following his death. However, historical records support only the Four Books as being the actual teachings of Confucius. His followers most likely authored the Five Classics.

The Four Books, also known as the Analects, are easily read and understood by those with only the most basic introduction to

Confucianism. The wisdom is timeless, focusing on many of the same topics covered in the I Ching. For this reason, I have found them to be an excellent resource for the purpose of creating a personal sacred text.

Thomas Cleary presents a beautiful translation in *The Essential Confucius: The Heart of Confucius' Teachings in Authentic I Ching Order.* He arranges the Analects according to the chapters of the I Ching, so that you can move easily from one sacred text to the other. If change is a topic you wish to cover in your sacred text, both the I Ching and the Analects are rich with material to choose from.

Hinduism

VEDAS

THE VEDAS, "wisdom" or "knowledge," are one of the oldest pieces of sacred literature in the world, dating to approximately 1550 B.C. Although they precede the formal development of the Hindu faith, they are commonly associated with it. This collection of legends, laws, rituals, and hymns, originally recited in Sanskrit, is thought to have been developed as a type of employment manual for Brahmin priests. There are four major Vedas: the Rig, Yajur, Sarma, and Atharva. They were first recorded in written form in about 600 B.C.

Notorious for their length (the Rig Veda alone totals 1,028 hymns) and difficulty, the Vedas are not widely available. Even if they were, most probably they would not be helpful for the purpose of creating a personal sacred text, as they focus on the rules and regulations governing sacrifices and ceremonies.

Selected portions of the Rig Veda are published in E. V. Arnold's translation titled *The Rig Veda.* It's difficult to read, and even after investing your time you may not gain much. If you want just a taste of it, see the listing for Zaehner's *Hindu Scriptures* later in this section.

UPANISHADS

THE 108 UPANISHADS are actually part of the Vedas, but because they are often published under their own titles I have provided this separate listing. They are the final portion of the Vedas that summarize the philosophy and wisdom contained in previous sections.

Because the Upanishads focus more on theoretical knowledge than law, they are much easier to read than the rest of the Vedas. It is still hard, though, to find complete manuscripts, and most translations are excerpts only. For the purpose of creating your personal sacred text this is fine. My favorite translation, for readability and commentary, is Juan Mascaro's *Upanishads*.

BHAGAVAD GITA

THE BHAGAVAD GITA ("Song of the Lord") is primarily a historical account of an epic battle. A great deal of the text is an ongoing dialogue between Krishna, the incarnation of the Hindu god Vishnu, and the warrior Arjuna. Composed during the fourth or third century B.C., it is the most widely known and translated Hindu text and is the second most translated sacred text behind the Bible. Espousing the virtues of duty, devotion, knowledge, and spiritual practice, the Bhagavad Gita frequently alternates between difficult and more accessible passages. Juan Mascaro's *Bhagavad Gita* is the simplest and least cluttered text.

EVERYMAN'S LIBRARY has published a nifty compendium of excerpts from these three texts in one volume titled *Hindu Scripture*. It has a portion of two Vedas and thirteen Upanishads, along with the Bhagavad Gita. While this translation is not necessarily the most readable one available, if you'd rather carry one book around than three, this is the selection for you.

· · ·

FOR AN EVEN SIMPLER introduction in a compact format, pick up Sri Chinmoy's *Three Branches of India's Life-Tree: Commentaries on The Vedas, The Upanishads, and The Bhagavad Gita.* Although, as the title states, it is intended to provide a discussion and not a recitation of the texts, it also contains excerpts. If you want to know more about the history and meaning of these Hindu scriptures, Chinmoy's book is an excellent resource.

Islam

QUR'AN

THE QUR'AN (commonly misspelled Koran) is the sacred text of the Islamic faith. Consisting of 114 chapters, it is believed to have been revealed to the prophet Muhammad by Allah between 610 and 644 B.C. Not unlike the Judeo-Christian sacred texts, the Qur'an, "The Recital," is composed largely of prophetic material and laws governing the behavior of its adherents.

Given the intertwining history of the Jewish, Christian, and Islamic traditions, the similarities between their sacred texts are not surprising. Muhammad believed himself to be a descendant of Ishmael, described in the Old Testament as the son of Abraham and the half brother of Isaac. Abraham's wife, Sarah, jealous of both Ishmael and his mother, raised a fuss and caused Ishmael to be exiled from the family while Isaac went on to become the revered father of the Israelite nation. The Qur'an communicates the belief that Jews and Christians were disobedient and were following false teaching. According to Muslims, the Islamic tradition began with the banished Ishmael, as Allah's attempt to redirect his chosen people.

I struggled with many translations before finding *Al-Qur'an: A Contemporary Translation* by Ali Jimale Ahmed and Ahmed Al. With the Arabic text on the left and the English on the right, this version is highly readable without compromising on the message contained in the original work. What used to be a chore is now a pleasurable read. Using this translation, I have found remarkable parallels between the Qur'an and other sacred texts, including the Dhammapada.

If this Islamic sacred text still seems too difficult, Thomas Cleary offers an abbreviated version in *The Essential Koran: The Heart of Islam*. It only provides excerpts, but the translation is simple and Cleary offers excellent commentary on the history and meaning of the Qur'an.

Judaism

TORAH

THE JEWISH TORAH is identical to the Old Testament portion of the Bible, previously described on page 80.

TALMUD

THERE ARE TWO VERSIONS of this Jewish sacred text, the Jerusalem Talmud and the Babylonian Talmud. The former was recorded in the late fourth century A.D. and the latter in the early sixth century A.D. Using legend, poetry, and storytelling, the Talmud provides comment on ancient Jewish custom, law, and daily life.

The Babylonian version is considered to be the most accurate and is consequently more widely studied. World-renowned rabbinical scholar Adin Steinslatz has done the best translation. For the text and an extensive commentary on its history and meaning, pick up one of his most popular works, *The Essential Talmud* and *Talmud, The Steinslatz Edition*, Vol. 10.

KABBALAH

THE KABBALAH (from the Hebrew root word *qibel*, meaning "to receive") focuses on the mystical teachings of Judaism. Although we know it is a collection of the most ancient wisdom within this tradition, it was kept secret for centuries, passed down only by oral transmission to those determined worthy of receiving its message. This has resulted, understandably, in difficulties documenting its history.

Legend holds that it was first taught by God to an exclusive group of angels, who then imparted it to the Old Testament characters Adam, Abraham, and Moses. It was finally recorded sometime around 580 B.C. by Rabbi Simen Ben Jochaim. Another significant portion was written by Moses de Leon and published in Spain in 1285.

The Kabbalah discusses such esoteric topics as interpretation of the Torah, moral purity, and relationship between mankind and the spiritual realm. The subject matter is somewhat similar to Buddhist texts that contemplate reality as an illusion and aim for transcendence to a higher level of consciousness.

Considered difficult to understand unless the reader is well versed in Judaism, the Kabbalah is only now beginning to be widely studied. I would add that it requires a love of philosophical and theoretical discussions to be fully appreciated. However, for readers with these traits, or if you just have a penchant to dive into a challenge, a good translation of the Kabbalah geared toward the modern reader is A. E. Waite's *Holy Kabbalah*.

Taoism

TAO TE CHING

THE TAO TE CHING, "The Way of Integrity," began, like many sacred texts, as an oral tradition. Legend states that the author was a wandering scholar by the name of Lao Tzu. Existing only by word of mouth from 650 to 350 B.C., it was finally recorded in written form sometime in the third century B.C.

The Tao Te Ching (pronounced Dow De Ching) is the third most translated sacred text, behind the Bible and the Bhagavad Gita. With eighty-one chapters, most under twenty lines, it is probably the shortest of all the works presented in this section. Written entirely in poetic verse, and rich in imagery, it is a beautiful text to both read and envision.

The best translation I've found is Victor H. Mair's *Tao Te Ching: The Classic Book of Integrity and the Way*. His work is eloquent and lyrical, and gives the reader an opportunity to interact with the text the way listeners would have centuries ago. It is also more accurate than any other translation because it is the first to be based upon the Ma-Wang-Tui manuscripts, which were discovered in 1973 and predate all other manuscripts by five hundred years. These older documents are much clearer and less contradictory than those other English translations were based on.

The Tao Te Ching is my favorite of all the sacred texts. Not only is it a pleasure to read, but it applies so readily to contemporary life. The wisdom about relaxing into the flow of life rather than fighting against it has carried me through many situations that would previously have thrown me into crisis. Consequently, I include many excerpts from it in my personal sacred text.

A great resource for transplanting the message of the Tao into our modern culture is *The Tao of Pooh* by Benjamin Hoff. When you become overwhelmed by the solemn nature of other sacred literature, reach for this book. You'll learn and laugh at the same time!

Anthologies

An Anthology of Sacred Texts By and About Women, edited by Serenity Young
This book is a must for every woman's library and a strong suggestion for men who wish to be their allies. It provides an in-

credibly diverse collection of literature from all the major faiths as well as lesser-known traditions, such as tribal and shamanistic religions. It may not be the most aesthetically pleasing volume, and its tiny, cluttered print strains the eyes, but it is the single most comprehensive anthology in the field of women's spirituality.

World Scripture: A Comparative Anthology of Sacred Texts, edited by Andrew Wilson
This volume was compiled by the International Religious Foundation to demonstrate the commonalities among the world's major religions. It is impossible to read this book and *not* believe in a River of Truth that flows beneath every faith tradition.

The World's Wisdom: Sacred Texts of the World's Traditions by Phillip Novak
This Bible for the world consists of excerpts from Buddhist, Hindu, Confucianist, Taoist, Jewish, Christian, and Islamic sacred texts. Novak adds a commentary for every selection that describes how each of these ancient traditions is lived with integrity in contemporary society.

Where to Begin

STILL FEELING OVERWHELMED and unsure where to start? Read the following descriptions. After selecting the category that most describes you, make your initial selection from the texts that accompany it.

BEGINNER

ARE YOU A novice who wants easily accessible translations of sacred texts? Try Kornfield's *Teachings of the Buddha*, Peterson's *The Message*, and any of the anthologies.

INTERMEDIATE LEVEL

DO YOU HAVE enough experience or courage to explore texts that delve a bit deeper and provide more insights to the world's religions but will still appeal to your Western sensibilities? Try Cleary's *The Dhammapada*, Robinson's *Nag Hammadi Library*, Dening's *Everyday I Ching*, and Mair's *Tao Te Ching*.

ADVANCED LEVEL

DO YOU LIKE to submerge yourself into foreign cultures and traditions? Try the Rhys-Davids' *Dialogues of the Buddha*, the Jesus Seminar's *Five Gospels*, Zaehner's *Hindu Scriptures*, and Waite's *Holy Kabbalah*.

Finding Resources

NOW THAT YOU'VE made your selections, where do you find them? My first recommendation is always your local library. You need to spend some time with a text before you will know if it is a good choice for you, and because books concerning major sacred texts can be very expensive, it's advisable to borrow before you buy. Other lending sources are churches and spiritual communities. Ministers and clergy usually have extensive private collections that they may allow you to peruse. Make sure to scout out the libraries of seminaries and colleges in your community too. And don't forget the Internet. Online resources are listed separately below.

To purchase a selection, try a large bookstore or one that specializes in religious and spiritual books. Most of the texts I recommend are not typically stocked on the shelves—there simply is not enough demand for them. However, it is rare that a bookseller will not order a title he or she does not have on hand. Or you can always get on the Internet and search the extensive website of Barnes & Noble (www.barnesandnoble.com). If it carries the title you want, it can usually ship within twenty-four hours.

Internet Resources

As you can imagine, the World Wide Web hosts a plethora of information about the world's sacred texts. There are sites that focus on one book or tradition and others that seek to span the globe.

A word of caution about sacred texts available on the Web: Accuracy can be a significant problem. Because posting information on the Internet is so easy, some individuals are offering translations that are actually nothing more than their personal, and often incomplete, interpretation of the original. A good rule of thumb is to stick to sites sponsored by reputable organizations. Check out the translator's credentials and beware of translations that differ dramatically from others of the same text.

I have found the following sites to be the most comprehensive and easiest to navigate:

http://webpages.marshal.edu/~wiley6/
This is a site sponsored by Marshal University and contains
most of the texts discussed in this chapter. The university has
a comprehensive collection of apocryphal texts (manuscripts
once considered part of the Bible, but excluded by the church
forefathers from the final compilations) from the Old and
New Testament eras.

http://scholar.cc.emory.edu/scripts/schol/:pev.html
Emory University maintains this extensive site. It not only publishes sacred literature but also lists journals, newsletters, and bibliographies about them.

http://www.gnofn.org/whsl/education/sacred.html
This website, oddly associated with the Greater New Orleans Free Net, offers an extensive listing of sources for finding information about sacred literature on the Internet. Links are provided so you can quickly locate each selection.

http://www.randomhouse.com/everymans
This is the online version of the Everyman's Library, sponsored by Random House publishing company. Most of the major sacred texts are represented. The site has well-developed search capabilities that allow you to look for verses, topics, dates, people, and places.

http://www.ipl.org
This is the website of the Internet Public Library. Under their Dewey decimal classification 200 they have an extensive collection of sacred texts associated with the majority of the world's spiritual traditions. The translations are top notch and the texts are complete, rather than excerpted or abridged.

http://religionworld.org/sacred.html
Although a Christian ministry by the name of Spring of Life Ministries sponsors this site, they do an excellent job of presenting introductory information to almost every world religion. Included are complete texts from the Zen, Hindu, Christian, and Islam faiths. This is a good site to sample some of the history and beliefs of a spiritual tradition along with its sacred text.

EIGHT

Other
Spiritual
Resources

THE SACRED TEXTS of the world's major religious traditions are not the only resources that discuss Spirit. A vast body of work not included in any of the material discussed in chapter 7 overtly references Spirit. These selections are as varied in genre and subject matter, spanning the same distance around the world and across time, as the sacred texts. They contain as much wisdom and insight too. The difference between these two categories lies only in where they ended up being recorded.

This chapter will help you locate and research the extensive collection of spiritual literature and artwork from around the world. It provides a number of subcategories that will help you understand the different genres of work available. Under each heading I have provided references to books or catalogs that I have used and recommended to my clients. I tried to include a variety of works that represent all spiritual traditions and at the same time are easily accessible and understandable to the introductory reader.

You may notice that a large number of the resources have the term "mystical" in the title or description. Because of the nature of this journey, I have found the writings of ancient and contemporary mystics to be particularly applicable. I highly recommend that you read some of those works. You will find them rich in possibility and remarkably representative of your own experience of creating your personal sacred text.

The number of choices and the information presented in this chapter may seem overwhelming. These resources merely represent opportunities to get to know Spirit better. They are not required reading. Take your time sorting through them. Explore an unfamiliar genre or tradition. Look up that book you've always wanted to read. Most important, have fun.

Devotionals and Meditations

THE MARKET IS FLOODED with books that provide daily devotional readings on virtually any subject you can imagine. There are selections for those in recovery, stay-at-home moms, and even pet lovers. Some are overtly spiritual or religious while others are targeted for a secular audience looking for inspirational material or an affirmation to begin their day.

Devotionals and meditations might be the perfect place for you to start your journey into spiritual literature. Because the individual selections are usually very brief, they will allow you to start with small bites. The lesson or message is typically very clear, making it easily applicable to your life.

> *Daily Word: Love, Inspiration, and Guidance for Everyone*
> Affirmations and meditations were collected from a year's worth of *Daily Word* (a Unity School of Christianity publication of daily devotions) magazines and compiled into this single volume. Although the accompanying scripture verses are from the Bible, the message is universal. I frequently use this

book when I travel because it is compact and versatile.
Because they are so simple yet powerful, several of the affirmations have made their way into my personal sacred text.

*A Deep Breath of Life: Daily Inspiration for Heart-Centered
Living* by Alan Cohen
Cohen teaches through storytelling. This book is filled with
humorous and touching vignettes that provide many layers of
wisdom. It is my favorite devotional, and I use it on a daily
basis.

My Utmost for His Highest by Oswald Chambers
This is a classic in the Christian tradition. Oswald Chambers
was a Protestant minister and dynamic speaker very popular
in England in the early 1900s. This is a collection of wisdom
based on biblical lessons culled from his lectures.

*Seeking the Path to Life: Theological Meditations on God and the
Nature of People, Love, Life, and Death* by Ira F. Stone
Rabbi Stone wrote this collection of meditations on contem-
porary issues in everyday language.

Simple Abundance: A Daybook of Comfort and Joy by Sarah
Ban Breathnach
Ban Breathnach has written an eloquent and wise collection
of devotionals directed at helping women simplify and return
the sacred to their everyday lives.

Essays

THIS IS A large and varied category. Unlike devotions and meditations, essays can be both lengthy and complex. Some of the anthologies listed have small excerpts from various authors on a particular

subject. Essays may be a good place to start your search. Don't feel obligated to take the entire essay or selection quoted by the author if only a paragraph or few sentences suit your needs.

Being Bodies: Buddhist Women on the Paradox of Embodiment, edited by Lenore Friedman and Susan Moon
This assemblage of essays by American Buddhist women about their experiences with spiritual enlightenment while occupying human bodies is a must read for anyone struggling with body size or image issues.

Buddhism in the West: Spiritual Wisdom for the 21st Century, compiled by Michael Tom
Tom has assembled a collection of writings by spiritual leaders, such as the Dalai Lama and Jack Kornfield, on the role of Buddhism in contemporary Western culture.

Communion: Contemporary Writers Reveal the Bible in Their Lives, edited by David Rosenberg
This anthology of essays describes the impact selected books of the Bible have had on the lives of thirty-six contemporary writers.

The Desert Fathers, translated by Helen Waddell
In the fourth century A.D., Christian men and women, retreating from what they felt was a corrupt society, moved into the deserts of North Africa and Asia Minor. Waddell has compiled and translated their writings into an easily understood volume that reflects the wisdom of the first Christian contemplatives.

Devotional Classics, edited by Richard Foster and James Bryan Smith
Foster and Smith have assembled the writings of fifty-two Christian mystics from various time periods. They have in-

cluded study questions and commentary that will help you understand the message and application of each excerpt.

The Enlightened Mind: An Anthology of Sacred Prose, edited by Stephen Mitchell
Mitchell, one of the most prolific contemporary translators of sacred literature, has created an anthology from the writings of spiritual leaders and thinkers of every tradition and time period. If you find this volume compelling, then refer to his companion works, *The Essence of Wisdom* and *The Enlightened Heart*, listed on pages 117 and 113.

For the Love of God, edited by Benjamin Shield and Richard Carlson
This book is comprised of essays written by contemporary spiritual and psychological thinkers, such as the Dalai Lama and Barbara Marx Hubbard, discussing their relationship with Spirit.

In the Spirit by Susan L. Taylor
Taylor, editor-in-chief of *Essence* magazine, has assembled a collection of her monthly columns that relate her interactions with, and the wisdom she receives, from Spirit.

The Inner Life by Hazrat Inayat Kahn
This volume contains three essays on the mystical, spiritual life of the Islamic Sufis.

Nature and Other Writings by Ralph Waldo Emerson
This collection of Emerson's essays includes many of my favorites, such as "Self-Reliance" and "Spiritual Laws." While any of Emerson's writings will be beneficial to your journey, I have found this compilation to be the best for creating a personal sacred text.

The Plain Reader by Scott Savage
This is a collection of essays by the editor of *The Plain Reader*,
a magazine that serves the Luddite, Amish, and Quaker communities. In our hectic and technologically advanced world,
Savage's compilation of the pleasures of a simple and communal lifestyle is a breath of fresh air.

*Sacred Stories: A Celebration of the Power of Stories to Transform
and Heal*, edited by Charles Simpkinson and Anne
Simpkinson
The Simpkinsons have assembled a remarkable collection of
contemporary authors, spiritual leaders, and popular personalities, such as Al Gore and Maya Angelou, who have written
about how specific spiritual stories have influenced their
lives.

*Search for the Meaning of Life: Essays and Reflections on the
Mystical Experience* by Willigis Jager
This is a collection of the author's lectures, essays, and personal reflections on various aspects of the mystical experience. Jager is a learned Benedictine monk from Germany
whose writing is both rich and deep. I have found his personal
reflections to be particularly meaningful and relevant to my
own journey.

*The Spirituality of Imperfection: Modern Wisdom from Classic
Stories* by Ernest Kurtz and Katherine Ketcham
This is the perfect book for those of you struggling to overcome perfectionism and come to peace with being imperfect.
Kurtz and Ketcham eloquently use stories from various
sources, such as the Greek philosophers and Buddhist sages,
to provide powerful spiritual guidance on how to leave your
struggles behind.

Teachings of the Jewish Mystics, edited by Perle Besserman
This collection of works is excellent introductory reading for
anyone unfamiliar with Judaism and seeking a place to begin
studying. It will give you a wonderful sampling of all the great
mystics from the Jewish tradition, helping you discern the
best path to explore next.

Visions and Longings: Medieval Women Mystics by Monica
Furlong
Furlong has assembled a collection of essays by eleven medieval Christian mystics. She has included the well known,
such as Hildegard of Bingen, and the lesser known, such as
Angela di Foigno. Her helpful commentary precedes each
selection.

Visions of God: Four Medieval Mystics and Their Writings,
compiled by Karen Armstrong
Armstrong provides excerpts from the writings of Richard
Rolle, Walter Hilton, Dame Julian of Norwich, and the
anonymous author of *The Cloud of Unknowing*, accompanied
by her own commentary. She has several other books that
you might enjoy, including the classic *A History of God*.

Weavers of Wisdom: Women Mystics of the 20th Century, edited
by Anne Bancroft
Many books contain the writings of mystics from centuries
ago. Bancroft has assembled a rare collection of work from
fifteen modern-day female mystics. She combines excerpts
from their work with her own eloquent and insightful commentary.

Hymns and Songs

MUSIC IS A powerful conduit of Spirit. It offers us a form of expression and interpretation that engages both the linear left brain and the creative right brain. Consequently, songs and hymns can have twice the power of communicating their message as the written word alone. I have found my clients' tastes in music to be so varied that I cannot possibly make adequate recommendations to them. Undoubtedly a song or artist comes to mind when you think about this category of selections. Start with that and explore outward.

The category of hymns may be a different story. Many of us grew up in traditions that sang what we felt were tired old hymns when we would rather have been enjoying something much more upbeat and contemporary. Consequently, it may be hard to imagine that those verses could have anything to offer of such significance that we would want to add it to our sacred text. Before you jump to that conclusion, check out the following references on hymns and the stories behind them. There is also a reference for nontraditional chants and ritual songs.

Amazing Grace: Hymn Texts for Devotional Use, edited by
Bertus Frederick Polman, Marilyn Kay Stulken, Bert Polman,
James R. Sydnor
This collection of hymns is arranged topically. Only the
words of the songs are included, but this will still allow you to
study their meaning and application.

Amazing Grace: 366 Inspiring Hymn Stories for Daily Devotions
by Kenneth W. Orbeck
Orbeck provides a fascinating description of the story behind
the writing of each hymn. This book is filled with tales of spir-

itual journeys, triumphs, and tragedies that will inspire you and give you a new appreciation of the songs included.

Circle of Song: Songs, Chants, and Dances for Ritual and Celebration, compiled by Kate Marks
Marks has created a wonderful book filled with the words and music to a variety of songs and chants suitable for use in movement exercises and rituals. Groups or individuals can use them to build community, promote healing, and celebrate life.

Facing the Music: Faith and Meaning in Popular Songs by Darrell W. Cluck, Catherine S. George, and J. Clinton McCann, Jr.
In this book the authors address the spiritual wisdom that can be found in secular contemporary music. They create a powerful argument for why songs that do not overtly refer to Spirit should still be considered as containing spiritual wisdom.

Inside the Music: Conversations with Contemporary Musicians about Spirituality, Creativity, and Consciousness by Dimitri Ehrlich
This unique book provides a perspective on contemporary, secular music rarely explored in today's society. Artists such as Mick Jagger, Al Green, and Ziggy Marley provide their reflections on the relationship between music and spirituality. If you find music to be a powerful spiritual medium, this is absolutely required reading.

Interviews

MANY CONTEMPORARY spiritual leaders and teachers have written books or created video- and audiotapes from which you can access their wisdom. For those who have not, books that summarize interviews or interactions with the great minds of our times can come in quite handy.

The Future of God: Personal Adventures in Spirituality with Thirteen of Today's Eminent Thinkers by Samantha Trenoweth
Trenoweth documents her interactions with various personalities, such as Bishop Desmond Tutu and the Dalai Lama, regarding their thoughts and beliefs about the future of spirituality and faith.

Inspired: The Breath of God by Joanna Laufer and Kenneth S. Lewis
Laufer and Lewis provide the reader with a view into their conversations with gifted minds, such as Thomas Moore and Madeleine L'Engle, about their faith and how it inspires their work.

Tying Rocks to Clouds: Meetings & Conversation with Wise and Spiritual People by William Elliott
Elliott has interviewed contemporary spiritual leaders, such as Elisabeth Kübler-Ross and Mother Teresa, regarding their ideas, philosophies, and experiences.

Legends, Stories, Myths, and Folktales

THE ORAL TRADITION of storytelling preceded any form of the written word. For this reason, myths and legends that originated from early eras carry a great deal of the world's earliest wisdom. In our contemporary society we rarely tap into these resources. Don't cheat yourself out of this vast storehouse of knowledge by skipping these.

Earthmaker: Tribal Stories from North America by Jay Miller
Miller has assembled the creation myths from various tribal civilizations that lived in North America.

Folklore, Myths and Legends: A World Perspective by Donna Rosenberg
Rosenberg, an expert in world mythology, retells thirty stories, from Greek myths to European folktales, in her own words. Her selections not only span the globe but the time line as well. Along with each story she provides background information and history that makes it all the more meaningful and understandable.

The Global Myths: Exploring Primitive, Pagan, Sacred, and Scientific Mythologies by Alexander Eliot
Myths from around the world, along with Eliot's commentary, are collected in this resource. You will find tales that originate from various sources, including ancient Greece, the Native American tradition, Hinduism, and ancient Asian cultures.

The Mythology of Native North America by David Leeming and Jake Page
This is an extremely readable and accessible volume of work that assembles the many myths of the Native American spiri-

tual tradition. In my opinion, it is the best collection of its kind on the market.

Sun Stories: Tales from Around the World to Illuminate the Days and Nights of Our Lives by Carolyn McVickar Edwards
Edwards has assembled a collection of twenty-six tales from around the world that focus on the role of the sun in our lives.

Voices of the Winds: Native American Legends by Margot Edmonds and Ella E. Clark
This is an anthology of more than 100 legends from Native American tribes sorted by their originating geographical region.

The Wisdom of African Mythology by John J. Ollivier
Ollivier provides an uncluttered book that relates African myths in simple prose, giving the reader insight into the culture and beliefs of African tribal life.

Memoirs, Biographies, and Journals

THIS IS MY favorite category. Because you are on a spiritual journey, memoirs and journals that focus on the same type of process will feel like eavesdropping on a familiar conversation. Reading these selections will give you courage, wisdom, and guidance for your own spiritual journey.

Collision with the Infinite by Suzanne Segal
Segal's spiritual autobiography relates her unexpected encounter with the infinite universe while waiting to catch a bus one day in France and her struggle to comprehend this event for years afterward.

Fragrant Palm Leaves: Journals 1962–1966 by Thich Nhat Hanh
This book provides a unique insight into the developing years of one of today's most respected spiritual leaders. Reading about the author's spiritual journey will provide wisdom and hope for your own.

A Jewish Mother in Shangri-La by Rosie Rosenzweig
Rosenzweig tells a wonderful story of her travels with her Buddhist son to various retreat centers around the world in an effort to understand his chosen spiritual path. Along the way she learns many lessons about her own Jewish faith and ends her travels in the city of her ancestors, Jerusalem.

Nine-Headed Dragon River: Zen Journals by Peter Matthiessen
Matthiessen discusses his search for spiritual roots in this intimate and painfully honest account of his journey toward becoming an ordained Buddhist monk.

Stalking Elijah: Adventures with Today's Jewish Mystical Masters by Rodger Kamentz
This is Kamentz's story of his search for meaning and understanding following the death of a child. His spiritual quest takes him all the way to India and results in a deeper understanding of and faith in his Jewish religion.

Surprised by Grace: A Journey Beyond Personal Enlightenment by Amber Terrell
A poignant story of one woman's spiritual quest for the elusive concept of enlightenment. After striving for years to find inner peace through meditation, she found it remained out of her reach. Only when she realized that enlightenment was something that resided within her, not something she

obtained through a spiritual practice, did she find the answers she was seeking. Although Terrell writes from a Vedic tradition, her journey is easily applied to anyone's search for wisdom and truth. This book so captured my attention that I read it cover to cover in one sitting.

General Nonfiction

THESE RESOURCES provide extensive introductions to or discussions of a particular aspect of spirituality. Unlike many of the prior listings, they are not set up for skimming through to find a specific meaningful passage. However, if you are interested in studying the topics they discuss in depth, these resources will meet that need.

The Druid Source Book by John Matthews
This book contains a history and collection of the wisdom of the Celtic Druids.

The Good Heart: A Buddhist Perspective on the Teachings of Jesus by His Holiness the Dalai Lama
The leader of the Tibetan Buddhist community has written an eloquent description of the commonalties between his spiritual tradition and Christianity.

Meister Eckhart, from Whom God Hid Nothing: Sermons, Writings, and Sayings, edited by David O'Neal
Meister Eckhart was an immensely popular Catholic priest who lived in the late thirteenth and early fourteenth centuries. Because he was eventually excommunicated for his heretical beliefs, these teachings were handed down in secret for many generations. His writings, especially the belief that everything contains Spirit, form the foundation of much of Western mystical tradition.

Teachings on Love by Thich Nhat Hanh
This is a beautiful and eloquent treatise about Buddha's
teachings on love.

*Toward a Meaningful Life: The Wisdom of the Rebbe Menachem
Mendal Schneerson*, adapted by Simon Jacobson
Jacobson relates the teachings of Rebbe Menachem, the head
of the Jewish Orthodox Lubavitcher movement for forty-four
years, regarding the application of ancient truths to contemporary life.

Wise Words: Jewish Thoughts and Stories Through the Ages by
Jessica Gribetz
This is a collection of ancient and contemporary Jewish
wisdom.

With Open Hands by Henri J. M. Nouwen
While I love all of Nouwen's work, this book about prayer
is my favorite. He eloquently captures the joys and struggles
of communing with Spirit. Beautiful photographs taken
by Ron Van Den Bosch and Theo Robert accompany the
text. The combination of words and images is particularly
powerful.

The Words of My Perfect Teacher by Patrul Rinpoche, translated by the Padmakara Translation Group
This classic is a practical guide to Tibetan Buddhism written
by one of the tradition's most respected teachers. Rinpoche
uses stories, quotations, and examples from daily life to make
his lessons easy to understand and accessible to every reader,
regardless of his or her faith background.

Poetry

POETRY, LIKE music, is doubly powerful in conveying its message because it taps into both our right- and left-brain processes. Some of you may have been turned off this genre because it has been difficult to understand or apply to your own life. Don't let that deter you now. The selections listed here contain work that is generally easy to understand. Start with one of the anthologies if you feel unsure about how or where to begin.

Beyond Self: 108 Korean Zen Poems by Ko Un
This collection from Korea's premiere Zen poet invites us to fully participate in every aspect of our lives.

Call Me by My True Names: The Collected Poems of Thich Nhat Hanh by Thich Nhat Hanh
This is a collection of 100 poems composed over forty years that focus on the author's journey from struggle and difficulty to celebration.

Claiming the Spirit Within, edited by Marilyn Sewell
This is a wonderful anthology of 300 poems by contemporary women writers. They are arranged by topic and subject. If you like this volume, seek out Sewell's earlier anthology: *Cries of the Spirit*.

The Clouds Should Know Me by Now, edited by Mike O'Connor and Red Pine
O'Connor and Pine have gathered a collection of poetry from fourteen Buddhist monks written over the last twelve centuries that eloquently express the essence of Buddhism.

The Enlightened Heart: An Anthology of Sacred Prose, edited by
Stephen Mitchell
This is Mitchell's companion to his earlier work, *The
Enlightened Mind*, which is listed under "Essays."

The Illuminated Rumi by Jalal Al-din Rumi, translated by
Coleman Barks, illustrated by Michael Green
This is a collection of work by the most popular of the Islamic
Sufi poets. Rumi's writing does a wonderful job of celebrating
the sacred in everyday life. Complete with illuminating illus-
trations, this is a beautiful book.

The Prophet by Kahlil Gibran
Gibran's classic discusses all of the topics relevant to today's
modern search for spiritual enlightenment, from giving, to relationships, to pain. This is a timeless work that you should at
least sample.

What Book? Buddha Poems from Beat to Hiphop, edited by Gary
Gach
This is an anthology of 330 poems from 125 contemporary authors. It is a fantastic representation of the variety of ways
many individuals can interpret and express their relationship
within the same spiritual tradition.

Prayers and Blessings

PRAYER IS THE universal language of believers of all spiritual traditions. Although the rote recitations of Catholic standards during
my childhood left me searching every other category except this one, I
found a new appreciation when I took the time to explore the works of
other faiths. I hope you will take the time to stop and sample some of

them as well. The resources in this category are varied in every facet imaginable. The following listings will give you numerous choices among length, genre, and complexity.

An African Prayer Book, edited by Desmond Tutu
Archbishop Tutu has gathered into one volume a collection of prayers originating from various aspects of African culture.

Between Heaven and Earth by Ken Gire
This anthology of work, mostly from the Christian tradition, includes prayers and writings about the theology and practice of prayer.

The Book of Blessings by Marcia Falk
This book provides new Jewish prayers for daily life, the Sabbath, and the New Moon Festival. Beautifully written in both English and Hebrew.

The Celtic Way of Prayer: The Recovery of the Religious Imagination by Esther DeWaal
DeWaal provides a beautiful introduction to the poetic and poignant Celtic tradition of prayer.

Prayer: Language of the Soul by Phillip Dunn
Dunn discusses the tradition, history, and theology of prayer followed by 300 selections.

Short Prayers for the Long Day, compiled by Giles and Melville Harcourt
This is a collection of prayers of Christian origin cataloged by subject and purpose.

Quotations, Sayings, and Proverbs

AFTER COLLECTING a variety of quotes that were short in length but immense in power, I started a section in my personal sacred text titled "Proverbs." I found it particularly helpful to commit those verses to memory so that they were accessible to me at any time. Several have become almost personal mantras that I repeat in the face of stress and pressure. Gathered here are numerous resources that will provide you with thousands of choices from various traditions and cultures.

Illuminating Wit, Inspiring Wisdom: Proverbs from Around the World, edited by Wolfgang Mieder
The world's foremost authority on proverbs has assembled a collection of 2,000 from various countries and time periods.

Oneness: Great Principles Shared by All Religions, compiled by Jeffrey Moses
Moses has taken brief scripture quotations from the sacred texts of the major world religions to demonstrate the common principles that they share.

The Quotable Spirit: A Treasury of Religious and Spiritual Quotations from Ancient Times to the 20th Century, compiled and edited by Peter Lorie and Manuela Dunn Mascetti
This anthology of excerpts from sacred texts, poetry, and prose represents the collective wisdom generated from centuries of spiritual exploration in a variety of traditions and faiths.

Quotations of Wit and Wisdom, compiled by John Gardener and Francesca Gardener
The Gardeners have created an exhaustive compilation of instructive and entertaining statements from ancient to present

times. They are divided topically, with subject headings such as education, change, and friendship.

Timeless Wisdom, compiled by Gary W. Fenchuk
This collection of quotations from a variety of sacred and secular sources is meant to represent humankind's most powerful truths, such as overcoming adversity or living life to the fullest.

Travelling the Path of Love: Sayings of the Sufi Masters, edited by Llewellyn Vaughn-Lee
This compilation of writings by Sufi authors from the ninth century to the present day describes the path of love that leads to Spirit.

Collections of Mixed Genre

SOME ANTHOLOGIES combine a variety of types of writing. Usually their aim is to illuminate a particular subject or spiritual tradition. I have personally used and recommended these to my clients:

Anam Cara by John O'Donohue
O'Donohue relates the ancient and timeless wisdom, poetry, and blessings of Celtic spirituality. The title is Celtic for "soul friend."

Catch the Whisper of the Wind, compiled by Cheewa James
Proverbs and short stories from the Native American tradition, written by various artists and leaders, are gathered in this book. While some are sad and some humorous, all relate the incredible wisdom carried within this ancient spiritual tradition.

Confirmation: The Spiritual Wisdom That Has Shaped Our Lives, edited by Kephra Burns and Susan L. Taylor
This is an absolutely beautiful book, in text and visual presentation. Burns and Taylor have gathered together the poetry, prose, and quotations that were instrumental in shaping their spiritual journeys and written commentary that explains why and how it affected them.

The Essence of Wisdom: Words from the Masters to Illuminate the Spiritual Path, edited by Stephen Mitchell
Mitchell's latest work provides excerpts from the works and words of the greatest spiritual leaders of all time that represent their central message and teachings.

God in All Worlds: An Anthology of Contemporary Spiritual Writing, edited by Lucinda Vardey
Vardey has assembled more than 100 writings in various genres by a wide variety of authors, such as Albert Einstein and Maya Angelou, seeking to express how they interpret and live the beliefs and values of their spiritual tradition.

God's Treasury of Virtues: An Inspirational Collection of Stories, Quotes, Hymns, Scriptures, and Poems
This is recognized as the classic anthology of spiritual writing and includes selections from virtually every era or corner of the world.

Heart Full of Grace: A Thousand Years of Black Wisdom, edited by Venice Johnson
This book is full of contemporary songs, poems, and essays on African American wisdom arranged by topical category.

The Heart of the Goddess: Art, Myth, and Meditations of the World's Sacred Feminine, compiled by Hallie Iglehart Austin
Austin has created a beautiful book that combines photographs, prayers, meditations, myths, and historical background on the sacred feminine with her commentary.

Heaven's Face Thinly Veiled: A Book of Spiritual Writing by Women, edited by Sarah Anderson
This is a wonderful anthology of essays, poetry, and fiction by women from all faith traditions celebrating Spirit. The authors range from medieval mystics to twentieth-century author Agatha Christie.

I Am with You Always: A Treasury of Inspirational Quotations, Poems, and Prayers, compiled by Douglas Bloch
Bloch has assembled a collection of material that represents every era from all faith traditions, including brief quotes and proverbs and lengthier poems or text excerpts. Items are arranged topically according to headings, such as "Providing for Your Needs" and "Healing Your Relationships."

Native American Wisdom, edited by Kent Nerburn and Louise Mengel Koch
This book provides excerpts of speeches and writings authored by members of many different Native American tribes.

Return of the Great Goddess, edited by Burleigh Muten
This is an absolutely beautiful anthology of poetry and prose celebrating the divine feminine across ancient and contemporary civilization. The gorgeous illustrations alone make investing in this book worthwhile.

The Spirit Mosaic: Women's Images of the Sacred Other, edited by Theresa King
Twenty-four women from various spiritual traditions have contributed to this anthology of prose, poetry, and interview. They focus on their concept of and relationship with the Divine. This eclectic work offers many different viewpoints in one volume, making it a good introductory selection.

Spiritual Literacy: Reading the Sacred in Everyday Life by Frederic and Mary Ann Brussat
The Brussats have gathered 650 excerpts from contemporary books and screenplays that demonstrate the presence of Spirit in material not typically interpreted as spiritual.

Storming Heaven's Gate: An Anthology of Spiritual Writings by Women, edited by Amber Coverdale Sumrall and Patrice Vecchione
This book contains sixty-one works of prose and poetry written by contemporary female authors of all faith traditions who seek to express a woman's sacred connection to Spirit.

Audio Recordings

SOMETIMES SPIRITUAL leaders and teachers record their messages rather than or in addition to writing them down. If you spend a great deal of time driving or listening to audiotapes, then this category may be an excellent way for you to do research for your personal sacred text. Although you may have to transcribe the words, such work will be nominal in exchange for the benefits you receive. There are two excellent resources for audio recordings of authors, leaders, and teachers from various traditions. Both can provide you with catalogs of their extensive collections:

New Dimensions Radio
P.O. Box 569
Ukiah, California 95482-0530
800-935-8273 in United States
707-468-9830 outside United States
www.newdimensions.org

Sounds True
P.O. Box 8010 Department W12
Boulder, Colorado 80306-8010
800-333-9185

Images and Visual Artwork

THE SELECTIONS you add to your personal sacred text do not have to be limited to the written word. Visual images are an excellent addition. They will provide you with a way to express feelings and concepts that you cannot put into words yourself or cannot find in someone else's writings. Consider making a color photocopy of the image if you do not have access to an original print or photograph. Huston Smith's *Illustrated World Religions* (referenced in chapter 7) has beautiful artwork from around the globe that captures the beliefs and values of the various spiritual traditions. Few other books have such a wonderful collection of images.

The Secret Language of the Soul: A Visual Expression of the Spiritual World by Jane Hope is a close second. This is an absolutely exquisite collection of commissioned artwork and photography that represents the different conceptions of soul in the world's spiritual traditions.

• • •

USE THESE RESOURCES as a starting point for your creative process. Explore what interests you. If you find a particular genre you really like, delve deeper into it with other authors and subjects. For specific instructions on how to make selections from the works you find have personal meaning for you, see chapter 10.

NINE

Secular
Resources

S PIRIT DOES NOT have to be mentioned or even indirectly referenced in every work you add to your personal sacred text. Truth is not only nondenominational but arises from a variety of sources, both spiritual and secular. It can be carried in the humor of a stand-up comedian or a letter from a woman to her husband fighting on the battlefield of a foreign land.

As you progress on this journey, you will find your ability to see Spirit's presence in any situation getting stronger. References will no longer need to be overt. You will be able to detect even the subtlest of traces leading to wisdom and truth. Soon you will be delighted by insight coming from every possible source in many different formats.

In my efforts to develop my open soul, I found that there was a point where I could find material everywhere I looked. For instance, when I was shopping for a new car, I visited a local Saturn dealership. Several days later the salesperson sent me a thank-you note for shopping there. It contained a listing of affirmations, one beginning with each letter of the alphabet, such as "Resolve to reflect on your life experience" and "Understand yourself in order to better understand others." Although these sayings did not directly reference Spirit, there was no denying that they reflected Spirit wisdom. I added several to the proverbs section of my personal sacred text.

In this chapter I won't be recommending as many resources as I did for the major sacred texts and the spiritual material, but I cover categories of potential material, providing examples so you can feel confident exploring on your own. Once you begin looking just in the sources you encounter in your daily life, such as bookstores and periodicals, you will find you have a wealth of choices.

Autobiographies and Memoirs

BOOKS THAT CONTAIN someone's life story and experience in his or her own words are typically rich sources of wisdom and inspiration. They don't have to be about the writer's spiritual quest, such as those I recommended in chapter 8, to yield potential selections for your personal sacred text. With your open soul (see page 41), you will be able to see evidence of Spirit in anyone's story, regardless of faith tradition or acknowledgment of the role of Spirit in his or her life.

While some autobiographies and memoirs cover the author's entire lifetime, others encompass shorter periods or only a specific issue. Do you have a favorite author, spiritual teacher, or public personality? Check to see if that person has written an autobiography or memoir and, if so, read it. You might just get an inspiring, rare glimpse into the private story behind the person's public behavior and thought.

If you are facing a particular issue, such as depression, look for a book written by someone about his or her encounter with the same thing. Autobiographies and memoirs address every possible subject, from aging, to eating, to childhood abuse. I have several books, for example, that I give to women facing the possibility or reality of breast cancer. At best these women gain insight; at the least they realize they are not alone in what they are thinking and feeling. The following are some examples of selections I used in creating my personal sacred text and recommended to my clients.

First You Have to Row a Little Boat: Reflections on Life and Living by Richard Bode
Bode has written a metaphorical tale that recounts his childhood sailing adventures and parallels them to lessons he has learned in his adult life. He addresses issues such as complacency, dealing with fear, and sorting through confusion.

A Message from God in the Atomic Age by Irene Vilar
After a suicide attempt, Vilar struggled to come to terms with her mother's suicide and her grandmother's imprisonment for murder. Her memoir, alternating between her journals and her family history, recounts her search for the truth and the creation of a new perspective of her past.

A Mythic Life by Jean Houston
Houston generously shares her life story in this autobiography. Through her first-person narrative, interspersed with ancient myths, we get a glimpse into the development of her belief system and teachings.

Seeing the Crab: A Memoir of Dying Before I Do by Christina Middlebrook
This is a powerful account of the author's battle with metastatic breast cancer. Her struggle to face and overcome a typically terminal illness yields enormous wisdom. Those who have faced or are facing a similar situation, either themselves or as a support person for a loved one, will find this book an invaluable resource.

Tuesdays with Morrie: An Old Man, A Young Man, and the Last Great Lesson by Mitch Albom
Albom spent fourteen Tuesdays with his mentor and former professor Morris Schwartz, while Schwartz was battling Lou Gehrig's disease. This book is filled with the wisdom and life lessons that were imparted to Albom during their time together.

Journals and Diaries

THIS IS MY FAVORITE secular resource. Perhaps there is a lot of voyeur in me, but I am absolutely fascinated by other journals and diaries. I love to read about how people perceived and chose to respond to the circumstances of their lives. Because most diaries and journals are not written with publication in mind, you get a rare uncensored and honest depiction of each author's thoughts and experiences.

Not only do these selections provide you with an opportunity to add material to your sacred text, but also they allow you to benefit from the lessons their authors have learned. You get the experience of their truth without having to put in all the work!

While almost any journal or diary will provide you with rich material, I have found the following to be particularly beneficial to my clients and me.

The Baby Boat by Patty Dann
This is Dann's diary account of her efforts to adopt a child from a foreign country after discovering that she and her husband were infertile. Couples and individuals who have faced this same heartbreaking diagnosis and journey will find this book to be a painfully honest reflection of their own process.

Between Two Streams: A Diary of Bergen-Belsen by Abel J.
Herzberg, translated by Jack Santcross
Herzberg was a prisoner for fifteen months in the Bergen-
Belsen concentration camp during World War II. These diaries, discovered upon his death in 1989, recount his thoughts
and experiences during his incarceration as he served in the
informal role of judge for his fellow prisoners.

Big Indian Creek: October 23–29, 1994 by Dave Hughes
For a week in 1994 Hughes retreated to the high desert
canyons in Oregon to fish in solitude and seek renewal. His
thoughts and reflections on the mysteries of life and death are
recorded in this book.

Journal of a Solitude by May Sarton
This is Sarton's first of many books to chronicle her lengthy
spiritual and artistic journey. This volume in particular discusses her retreat into solitude when her writing lost the
power and meaning it had previously held. Alone, she questions and seeks until she finds new answers and motivations.
If you like it, you should look for her subsequent work.

Journals of Sylvia Plath by Sylvia Plath, edited by Frances
McCullough and Ted Hughes
Plath, a brilliant poet who eventually took her own life,
writes of her internal and external struggles. This memoir will
prove helpful to those who have faced the emotional pain of
depression or another mental illness.

Revelations: Diaries of Women, edited by Mary J. Moffat and
Charlotte Painter
Moffat and Painter have compiled excerpts from the diaries of
women, both famous and unknown, that reveal their most in-

timate thoughts. The entries are at once honest, painful, and humorous to read.

Biographies

BIOGRAPHIES HAVE many of the same attributes as autobiographies and memoirs. Yet because a third person tells the story, I often find them to lack some of the vibrancy and depth of memoirs, journals, and autobiographies. When a story is filtered through another's perception, it is almost always altered, regardless of how hard the author tries to be objective. To avoid this, some biographers focus on recounting the facts of the subject's life rather than their ideas and thoughts. While this may provide valuable insight into how they arrived at their ideas, it seldom provides material you would want to include in your personal sacred text.

However, this does not render the entire category useless. Some biographers include excerpts from the subject's journals, lectures, and letters or have conducted such extensive interviews that they can provide remarkably accurate insights. If an autobiography of your favorite figure is not available, look for a biography that goes beyond the facts and delves into the person's thought processes and private behavior.

After Midnight: The Life and Death of Brad Davis by Susan Bluestien Davis
This is Bluestien Davis's account of the life of her husband, actor Brad Davis, including his struggle with drug addiction and his eventual death due to AIDS. This powerful narrative confronts many of our societal stereotypes about HIV, drug use, and the culture of Hollywood.

A Beautiful Mind: A Biography of John Forbes Nash, Jr. by Sylvia Nasar
John Forbes Nash, Jr., was a brilliant mathematician whose genius caught the world off guard when he was in his early

twenties. But his mental health deteriorated until he was eventually institutionalized due to schizophrenia. This biography tells the story of his rise to fame, descent into mental illness, and recovery to become a Nobel Prize winner in Economics in 1994.

Letters and Correspondence

LIKE JOURNALS and diaries, letters and correspondence are often quite revealing of authors' otherwise closely guarded thought processes. You may have to wade through mundane pleasantries or references to unknown characters, but your patience will be amply rewarded. Many books consist almost solely of letters written between lovers or during wartime. These are some good choices to explore.

Celebrating Success: Inspiring Personal Letters on the Meaning of Success, edited by Garard Smith
This book contains 150 letters from some of the world's most influential people relating their personal definitions of success.

800 Years of Women's Letters, edited by Olga Kenyon
Kenyon has compiled letters from women of every social strata and era over the past 800 years. They are organized by theme for easy reference.

Letters of a Nation: A Collection of Extraordinary American Letters, edited by Andrew Carroll
This is a wonderful collection of more than 200 letters written by Americans over the course of 350 years. They cover subjects ranging from love, slavery, war, social concerns, to death and dying.

Letters to a Young Poet by Rainier Maria Rilke, translated by
M. D. Herter Norton
Rilke wrote these letters between 1903 and 1908, before he
gained fame and attention as a poet. In an effort to pass along
what he had learned about life and the creative process, Rilke
wrote them to a young student who had sought his advice.

Essays

THIS IS A rich and varied category. Many prominent thinkers and
leaders have published collections of essays that contain both their
well- and lesser-known teachings. Some are highly theoretical while
others illustrate a particular principle through a metaphor or real-life
story. You will be able to find selections that discuss every imaginable
subject in a wide variety of formats. If you just want to sample an author's work or want to explore a topic through short readings rather
than wading through an entire book, essays are an excellent choice.

Altogether Elsewhere: Writers on Exile, edited by Marc
Robinson
This is a poignant and insightful collection of essays written
by various authors about their experiences in exile, either by
choice or by force. Although you may not be living in the
same situation, you will be able to identify with the themes of
solitude, allegiance, and divided loyalties.

Civil Disobedience and Other Essays by Henry David Thoreau
If you haven't read anything from Thoreau, this short collection of his classics is a good place to start.

High Tide in Tucson: Essays from Now or Never by Barbara
Kingsolver
Kingsolver, a noted fiction writer and essayist, has written an
eclectic mixture of pieces on topics ranging from motherhood
to environmental issues. I love Kingsolver's work. She's articulate, upfront, and remarkably insightful.

Fiction

PERHAPS YOU have not considered works of fiction as a resource
for material for your personal sacred text, but this category contains
remarkable wisdom. Many authors use allegories, satire, and other
forms of metaphor to convey their message. You may have to put more
thought into these readings, but it will be worth the effort. The variety
that fiction can bring to your text is also a significant strength.

Your fiction selections are not limited to works written for adults.
Children's books offer a wealth of wisdom as well. The following are a
few choices from both categories.

Aesop's Fables, edited by Jack Zipes and illustrated by J. J.
Grandville
This is a collection of Aesop's best-known fables, from "The
Country Mouse and the City Mouse" to "The Fox and the
Grapes," beautifully illustrated by the nineteenth-century
French artist J. J. Grandville.

Jonathan Livingston Seagull: A Story by Richard Bach
Bach's classic book is an allegory of a seagull and his quest to
attain perfect flight.

Jump Up and Say! A Collection of Black Storytelling, compiled by Linda Goss and Clay Goss
The Gosses have created an anthology that represents the rich wisdom inherent in the African American culture.

Poetry

UNLIKE STRAIGHTFORWARD prose, poetry speaks a language that supplies the senses with a banquet of information. Through its imagery and rhythmic verse, it propels us out of our strictly linear thinking into a world rich with metaphorical meaning. Poetry allows our creative-thinking skills to spring into action, helping us to make sense of concepts and ideas that our rational thought processes could not comprehend. Don't let prior bad experiences with poetry deter you from pursuing it in your creative process. The following resources are good places to seek poetry selections for your text.

Committed to Memory: 100 Best Poems to Memorize, edited by John Hollander and Eavan Boland
Because I am a great proponent of memorizing selections entered into your personal sacred text, I have found this resource invaluable. It has a nice variety of poems from which to choose, all short and simple enough to attempt to remember word for word.

World Poetry: An Anthology of Verse from Antiquity to Our Time, edited by Katharine Washburn, John S. Major, and Clifton Fadiman
This is the most comprehensive collection of poetry from all cultures and periods that I have encountered. I recommend it consistently as the best starting point for exploring the world of poetry.

Self-Help

TODAY'S MARKET is absolutely saturated with self-help material. It is tempting to find a book that can diagnose our troubles and provide a ready solution. Unfortunately, a lot of the answers we'll find in those books are misguided, uninformed, or even destructive. If the theory behind the advice as well as the guidance itself is unhealthy, chances are it will not be very useful.

For this reason I very seldom recommend self-help books to my clients in my therapy practice. I also always caution clients about using selections from this category in their personal sacred text. I would much rather that people decide for themselves what is at the root of their struggles and customize their own solution, knowing that great wisdom will come from both the process and the end result.

However, this does not mean that all self-help materials are useless. If you would like to explore this category, remember to scrutinize and examine everything you read through rather than accepting it at face value, regardless of the author's credentials or the popularity of the title. These titles are a few of the choices that support the empowering philosophy of creating a personal sacred text.

Finding True Love by Daphne Rose Kingma
Seldom is the search for a mate examined on such a spiritual level. Kingma has written a beautiful book on relationships that will give you a perspective of great wisdom and depth.

Seven Habits of Highly Effective People by Stephen Covey
This is a popular book often used by businesses to teach their employees time management and customer service strategies. However, it is rich in spiritual wisdom that will aid every aspect of your life.

A Whistling Woman Is Up to No Good: Finding Your Wild Woman by Laurel King
King has written a powerful guidebook for women seeking to live out their lives freely and fully in a society that does not always honor strong females.

Your Erroneous Zones by Wayne Dwyer
This classic book provides insight into the destructive patterns in our lives and the damage they cause. In an insightful and sensitive manner Dr. Dwyer provides the wisdom you need to correct those thoughts and behaviors and replace them with healthier ones.

Periodicals

THIS IS A wonderful category in which to find a sampling of every other type of resource mentioned in this chapter. You will find interviews, essays, poems, stories, and images on an endless array of subjects in the several thousand periodicals available to the general public, not to mention those printed for private organizations. If you are looking for publications that address the search for wisdom and truth, I suggest you explore:

Common Boundary
Conscious Living
Cross Currents
New Age Magazine
The Quest
The Shambhala Sun
Unity Magazine
The Utne Reader
The World

Humorous Material

LAUGHTER IS NOT only the best medicine, it is also a powerful conduit of insight and truth. Through a variety of circumstances in my life, I have realized that Spirit has an incredible sense of humor, a quality humankind has been gifted with as well. Although society at large may seldom consider anything with a punch line to be very spiritual, by now you have realized that Spirit can use any format to convey her message. Do not, therefore, overlook sources such as comic strips, editorial cartoons, and comedic performances or skits as possible sources of material for your personal sacred text.

I have two comic strips in my text. One is from Garfield about simple and profound truth. The other is from the now-defunct Calvin and Hobbes, who are discussing the paradox of sense and nonsense in today's culture. Both are among my favorite portions of my text and provide a wonderful change of pace from some pretty serious selections. One of my clients has an excerpt from a stand-up comedy routine performed by The Mommies, while another chose part of Bill Cosby's book *Fatherhood*. Spirit is present everywhere, speaking to us at all times. Keep your open soul radar on constantly, even during life's humorous moments.

Images

AS I STATED in chapter 8, your sacred text selections need not be limited to the written word. Imagery of any kind is not only welcome, it is needed. Words simply cannot capture some concepts, ideas, or experiences. Others can be written about, but a photograph or picture can provide the enhancement or expression needed to bring a concept to life. Remember, this process of creating a personal sacred text is a mystical one. To involve yourself with it completely you need sensory involvement, which the written word can begin to provide but only images will complete.

Seek photographs, prints, drawings, paintings, and collages to augment your text. Buy postcards at art museums or photocopy images from books. Create your own artwork. Ask a friend who is an artist to make something for you. An acquaintance of mine had a dream that gave her a beautiful metaphor for her spiritual journey. She asked her sister, who painted in watercolors, to re-create two scenes for her sacred text. They are among her most prized entries. Words would have been inadequate to capture what those two images conveyed. Explore your own methods of building your personal sacred text into a mystical adventure through the addition of imagery. Remember to include the appropriate documentation for each selection.

Lectures and Other Presentations

MOST OF US have spent more than a few hours attending workshops, classes, and other presentations for both personal and professional reasons. The message shared in these forums is often a source of wisdom to add to your sacred text because typically it is focused on education and growth. Keep your ears open during conferences and seminars. If you hear something you like, check to see if the presentation is being taped for sale afterward. Perhaps the speaker has written a book or articles that you can buy or reference. Or you can always take notes and reconstruct the message later at home.

My church tapes services and makes them available immediately afterward. As a result I have added several excerpts from the Sunday sermons to my sacred text. Doing so requires that I transcribe the portion I like, an act that usually causes me to put careful thought into my selection rather than deterring me from the task altogether. One of my clients copied a selection from a transcript of a workshop on childhood sexual abuse because it so closely echoed her experience as a survivor.

Another pasted her notes from a college lecture on the philosophy of Martin Buber into her text. You need not write out the message word for word; include enough text to jog your memory now and years in the future.

❧❦❧

Movies, Television, and Theater

LIKE OTHER categories in this chapter, scripts for television, movie, and theater performances are seldom seen as sources of spiritual wisdom or truth. However, my clients and I have amassed quite a collection of excerpts from plays and screenplays that indicate their worth. When I saw the movie *The Apostle*, I was awed by the scene where Robert Duvall's character rages against God about the injustice of his life so loudly that it wakes the neighbors. While I have never done exactly that same thing, I certainly have wanted to. My sacred text also has quotes from both *Gandhi* and *The Wizard of Oz*.

The Motion Picture Prescription by Gary Solomon is a wonderful resource for finding material from movies. He wrote the book for therapists and those in the process of healing and recovery, but anyone will find it useful in the process of creating a personal sacred text. He provides a synopsis of 200 movies along with what he feels are the primary lessons contained within them. There are both alphabetical and categorical indexes, making the material very accessible. All of the movies are available on video.

One of my clients regularly sets her video recorder to tape the *Oprah* show because she has found it to be a consistent source of material to add to her sacred text. Others have taken excerpts from episodes of *Touched by an Angel*, *Christy*, and even *Home Improvement*. Theater performances are also rich sources.

Songs and Music

MUSIC, LIKE imagery, is a vital part of your personal sacred text. It will convey your message in ways that words alone cannot. Wherever you listen to music, keep your ears open to the lyrics, the way the song makes you feel, or the image it brings to mind. I have scribbled down the words to more than one tune as I was driving down the highway. While listening to a country music station—not usually my typical choice—on a long road trip, I heard three different songs that I pulled over to record lyrics from.

One of my favorite haunts has become the large music store at the local mall where I can listen to any recording I want without having to buy it. I'm sure the salespeople find me quite annoying as I sit at the counter copying down lyrics from song after song.

Your selections can be solely instrumental or combine both lyrics and accompaniment. Include your choices in your text by inserting either a tape recording or the sheet music. Either is fine, depending on which is more meaningful to you. Don't forget to document your selections as outlined in chapter 5.

Objects

DON'T HESITATE to include small items, such as pressed flowers, a seashell, or a feather, that remind you of a particular encounter with Spirit wisdom. Place them into an envelope or a zippered pouch that you can tuck into the back of your text. Make sure to include documentation with each item, just as you would with a written selection. My text has a napkin from a dinner I attended where I heard someone talk about the use of poetry in her spiritual practice. I also have included a pair of earrings from a friend who gave me a wealth of wisdom about the use of creative expression in my life. One client keeps a packet of sand from the beach she visited the day she decided her life was worth living after years of battling drug addiction and anxiety. Just remember: Whatever you choose to include you must carry around for the rest of your life, so don't select anything too heavy or bulky!

FINDING SELECTIONS that are meaningful to you among secular literature and artwork will provide excellent exercise for your open soul. The more you explore, the greater capacity you will develop to see the sacred in everyday life. Use your expanded vision to delve deeper into particular subject areas or spiritual concepts that interest you. For assistance making selections that you will add to your personal sacred text, see chapter 10.

TEN

Selection
Guidelines

AT THIS POINT, given all of the resources you have been presented within the last three chapters, the process of determining what to add to your personal sacred text may appear somewhat daunting. So many options exist. You may feel yourself pulled in many different directions and focused in none. Don't be discouraged. I assure you that these are all normal experiences for this stage in the process. In this chapter you will find all the tools you need to help narrow your search and make wise choices about the pieces you will add to your text.

The selection process has two parts. First, you need to choose where to look for material that might yield an excerpt worth including. Second, you need to decide what, if any, portions of that work you will actually add to your text.

The first process is relatively simple and without much structure. Making that initial selection may seem the hardest part. I have had several clients get stuck at this point because they couldn't decide where to start. Keep in mind that there is no right or wrong way to begin the process. Choose something, anything, to break the ice. While I'm not advocating that you begin the process haphazardly, choose something that piques your curiosity and step forward into it. That selection will give you an idea to look somewhere else, and that resource will lead you to another. After a while the journey becomes self-perpetuating.

You may wish to begin by exploring something from the last three chapters that captured your attention. An anthology is always a good initial choice because it gives you a variety of authors and writing styles to sample. Or seek out a work that sparked your interest in the past. I had always wanted to read the Tao Te Ching because a friend had raved about it for years. I had resisted because the spiritual community I belonged to for so long discouraged exploring Eastern religious traditions. Once I freed myself from those restrictions, the Tao was the first book I rushed to buy. Perhaps you have a book or author that you have been waiting to explore as well but need permission or a reason to do so. Well, now you have both, so go for it!

You also can look around you for resources in your daily life. Is a coworker or friend reading a book that seems interesting? Attend lectures and presentations that intrigue you. Go to book readings and signings. Wander the libraries and bookstores. Surf the Web. Check out unusual places too, such as the comics or the dialogue from your favorite movie. Once you develop your open soul, you will see potential everywhere.

After you begin reading and exploring, you will need to tackle the second half of the selection process: deciding what pieces to add to your sacred text. The most important guidance I have for you here is simply to *be very selective*. Remember that this is a book you can take your time creating. There is no deadline to meet that requires you to make all of your selections quickly. If you load up on choices in the first few weeks or months, not only will the text become too cumbersome but it will also be difficult to use and integrate into your life.

Collecting too much too fast is easily the most frequent mistake I see my clients make. While you should not be afraid to add pieces to your text, you should do so with great care and consideration. Include something in your text only after carefully, deliberately, and consciously reflecting on its sacred nature.

Given that warning, let's take a close look at the tools you can use to make that kind of deliberate and wise choice.

Does It Meet the Definition of Sacred Art?

Do you remember the definition of sacred art, and specifically sacred text, that I presented in chapter 1? To fit into this category, a selection should create a triangular relationship among yourself as the reader, Spirit, and the author. The piece should give you an insight into Spirit that fits with your conception of who he is while at the same time revealing a communion between the author and Spirit that enriches your own experience with him.

When I conduct workshops, I typically ask participants to read some of their selections aloud to the group. It is not unusual for someone to share something that has the rest of the members shaking their heads, failing to see how it relates to Spirit. Yet when the person explains the relationship among him- or herself, the author of the piece, and Spirit, it rapidly becomes clear to the rest of us why it is an excellent selection. A poem read by someone about a mystical grocery shopping trip for the ideal apple might be meaningless to you or me, but it might perfectly capture the thoughts and feelings of someone on a spiritual journey seeking a vision for the future.

This definition of sacred art eliminates anything that is too complex or abstract for you to understand. For example, while I may find a poet's description of becoming a beetle and interacting with the world fascinating, that piece probably would not end up in my sacred text because I can't relate to the experience or the message.

Self-Awareness

IN ORDER TO KNOW what selections will be most beneficial for you, you must have some knowledge of who you are and what role Spirit plays in your life. This doesn't mean that you have to be wholly evolved and aware before you begin, but without some initial idea of self-concept, you will have nothing on which to base your selection decisions. Working on your sacred text without an idea of who you are is like grocery shopping without knowing what kinds of foods you like. Not only will you have a hard time deciding what to buy, but you also may end up throwing out a lot once you discover it doesn't suit your taste.

Susan came to our fourth workshop session still not having started her sacred text. The process had been frustrating for her, and she couldn't seem to settle on a place to begin. On the break we talked for a while about why she thought this was happening. She related that she had recently divorced and felt generally adrift in her life, wondering who she was and where she was headed. Self-knowledge is an important fuel that the creative process needs to maintain its forward motion. I encouraged her to take the time to explore her self-identity and vision for the future, reassuring her that once she made some headway into those areas, the process of selecting pieces for her sacred text would become much easier.

Before or during the creation process, take time to reflect. Journal, talk to a friend, read about personal growth and discovery, take a class, or begin a spiritual practice in your effort to define and refine your self-awareness. Use what you learn as a compass to guide the selections you add to your personal sacred text.

Intuition

EACH OF US has an intuitive process hard-wired into our right brain. It is a biological reality. Intuition is that sensation you feel when you know something despite not having any concrete facts to tell you why. I have heard several people refer to the intuitive process as one that allows us to make a wise decision based on insufficient information. We may experience our intuitive "knowing" in different ways, with a knot in our stomach or a tingle down our spine, but we all have the capacity to access this information.

As you read and research, one of your best guides in the selection process will be your intuition. If you are not experienced in listening to your intuition, you'll have to practice. When you read a piece that has some appeal to you, mentally note your initial response—describe the physical, emotional, or intellectual perceptions you have. I have found that intuition is often that immediate reaction you have when you encounter something. If it is a positive reaction, take the opportunity to follow that initial prompting. If you are still happy with the selection several days or weeks down the road, then chances are you have discovered the intuitive power of your right brain. Go back and review those initial notes you made and look for patterns in your responses. Once you've discovered how your intuition typically reveals itself, you'll be better able to recognize it in the future.

Spirit Guidance

JOHN WESLEY, theologian and founder of the Methodist denomination, wrote about a sensation he called a "strangely warmed heart" that told him Spirit was present and active in a believer's life. This is different from our intuition, as it is a spiritual process rather than a neurological response from our right brain. The patterns that you see repeating themselves in the intuitive process will probably not be evident when you tap into Spirit's guidance. She does not necessarily work in that kind of predictable way. A still, small voice may guide you one day, but the next day wisdom may come in the form of a friend's advice.

In his description Wesley seems to be referring what many Westerners would refer to as the presence of the Holy Spirit. Whether you believe in that particular aspect of Spirit or not, everyone has the power to tap into Spirit's guidance for making wise selections. When you find something that you think might make a good addition to your text, stop a moment and ask Spirit for input. Then listen carefully for a response.

When I was reading the Upanishads for the first time, I fell in love with the poetic lyrics. But for weeks I struggled to find a particular selection to add to my text. I sought Spirit's help but didn't think I received a response. Just when I was about to abandon the task, an excerpt from the Katha Upanishad turned up as the Sunday reading at church. It was perfect and I knew in an instant that this was Spirit's way of telling me what passage to select. Coincidences like these are seldom random; rather they are part of a divine plan to provide us with everything we need.

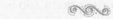

The Tao of Selection

THE BASIC TENETS of Taoism promote a serene and peaceful process of floating in life's current wherever it may take you. Forcing a particular outcome or demanding a change to suit your wishes is counterproductive because it takes you out of the best and highest possible good the universe has to offer. Apply this concept to your selection process. If it feels too contrived, awkward, or forced, chances are high that you are on the wrong path. Choose instead to follow the path that seems to lead naturally from one resource and reference to another. Trust the process and eventually it will lead you to the best selection.

When I feel I have to find something about a particular subject *now*, I will always come up empty-handed. If I'm feeling frustrated or the process of creating my sacred text seems flat, those are both clues for me to stop and put the process aside for a while. My best selections consistently come from serendipitous discovery rather than contrived circumstances.

Variety and Balance

THESE ARE TWO important elements to keep in mind as you make your selections. Don't overload your text with too many pieces from any one author, genre, subject area, or viewpoint. Because I have had so much loss in my life, it has been very tempting for me to make selections that reflect this theme. I constantly find poems, songs, and stories that say, once again, "exactly what I feel." Yet I've found that including too many pieces that center on these experiences leads to my building a very depressing sacred text—one I didn't even want to pick up and read! I have had to be very diligent and ask myself if a new selection is really necessary. Before you choose to include a selection, check to see if it repeats an aspect of a theme you have already covered or creates an uneven load among your variety of genres, viewpoints, and traditions.

Timeless Versus Transient Wisdom

WHEN YOU ARE considering what to add, look for timeless versus transient wisdom. Circumstances may arise in your life that will steer you deep into a particular subject. Following a dramatic weight loss, I collected almost twenty pieces about body image and size. Years later, outside of the immediate power of that victory, I found many of the selections to be meaningless. Without my notes to tell me why I had made some of the choices, I would not have remembered their significance—a clear indication that some of the selections needed to be removed. I didn't eradicate the entire category, because the issue of body image continues to be present in my life, but I did pare down the number and kept only those I felt had wisdom relevant to my overall experience as a soul temporarily housed in a human body. You too will want to refrain from making many selections during such times; items may be relevant in the moment, but they will lose their value later on because they are so situationally specific.

Speed of Selecting

YOU CAN MAKE selections for your sacred text immediately or after a lengthy period of consideration. The first time you read a piece you may instantly decide to include it. At the other end of the spectrum is a recognition that does not arrive until years after you first read the work. Most of your experiences will fall somewhere in between.

I distinctly remember the first time I had an experience with immediately and intuitively knowing something should be added to my text. I was sitting alone in my sister's living room late one night after everyone else had gone to bed. The television was tuned to *The David Letterman Show*, but I wasn't paying much attention to it. It was intended more to keep me company than hold my attention, as I was reading a new novel by one of my favorite mystery writers. Although I took vague notice of Dave introducing a singer, I quickly disengaged again when I discovered it was Sinead O'Connor. I had never been particularly fond of her work, even though that opinion was unfairly based on my knowledge of only a few songs. In my prejudice I paid scant attention.

Suddenly, despite my dismissal and involvement in my novel, the lyrics of her song were hitting my ears. Before my brain had fully registered what they were, my heart and soul had already summoned a knowing that they were powerfully suited to my journey. My book dropped unnoticed as I sat forward, intent on not missing one more nuance of this song. Tears flowed down my face as I listened to the words of a mother's unconditional and accepting love, even through our mistakes and our loneliness. I instantly knew this was something that needed to go in my personal sacred text—there was not a shred of doubt. It poignantly captured the essence of a maternal Spirit's love that superseded and encompassed the struggles of my own journey. If I could have run out in the middle of the night to buy a recording of that song, I would have. Several days later I was finally able to find the cassette tape and copied the words into my text the same day.

But not all selections will come with such speed. When I was in high school I took an American Literature class that exposed me to a variety of poetry and prose. Ella Wheeler Wilcox's work entitled "As If by Fire" (see page 56) was one of my assigned readings. In that moment it was not particularly meaningful to me. But years later, during my own spiritual struggles, my soul remembered it. I added it to my text more than a decade after my initial reading.

NO MATTER HOW you've made your selections—with an immediate knowing or a labored decision through time—it is wise to consider them, at least for a while, as temporary. Tuck them into your sacred text but don't officially add them until some time has passed—a few days at least, but more than a few weeks isn't necessary. After several reviews, if the piece still seems relevant and appropriate, then go ahead and include it permanently in your text. Remember that you always can remove something at any time in the future.

PART FOUR

Writing
Your
Own Scripture

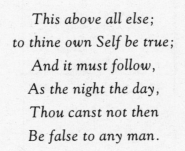

This above all else;
to thine own Self be true;
And it must follow,
As the night the day,
Thou canst not then
Be false to any man.

— WILLIAM SHAKESPEARE

ELEVEN

Writing
Your
Own Scripture

COLLECTING EXCERPTS of others' work is only part of the process of creating a personal sacred text. Writing your own scripture is the other part. For your book to be truly a reflection of you, it needs to be infused with your own words—ones that relate your own experience with spiritual truth. Without this, your sacred text will be reduced to a simple anthology of writings on spirituality.

Your scripture can take many forms, from poetry, to essays, to short stories. It will tell of your spiritual journey and the wisdom you encountered along the way. For example, after a period of feeling disconnected from Spirit, I wrote a prayer that I have included in my personal sacred text. It includes these lines: "Shine brightly for it seems my eyes are blind, / speak loudly for I am feeling deaf, / and reveal yourself clearly for I am surrounded by confusion." I could just as easily have used these thoughts to prompt a poem, essay, or set of proverbs as I did a prayer. The subjects or formats that you can explore in your scripture writing are vast. You need only take a quick tour of the types of writing and subject matter in the various sacred texts covered in chapter 7 to see the opportunities available to you.

Writing your scripture itself has two parts: receiving wisdom from Spirit and putting that wisdom into written form. Both are essential pieces and deserve careful attention. Chapter 12 addresses how to tap into Spirit's inspiration, and chapter 13 outlines the process of writing your scripture. Before you begin either one of these elements, though, it is important for you to understand why you need to write your own scripture.

Receiving Wisdom from Spirit

RECEIVING WISDOM from Spirit seems to be the most difficult mission for people to complete. I have had clients work on their personal sacred text for years before they start writing their own scripture, no matter how much assistance and reassurance I offer. Their reluctance seems to stem from two concerns: Once they were taught that only saints and prophets wrote scripture, and they don't think they have the necessary talent. Let me tell you why neither of these reasons is applicable.

Many Western spiritual traditions teach that the Bible is the infallible and inspired word of God. They believe scripture contains the perfect law and direction of Spirit to his followers. Some believe it should be interpreted literally, meaning that the story of Noah and the Ark is a record of an actual historical event. Others believe that the Bible is a mixture of literal and metaphorical writings, that the New Testament contains largely historical records while portions of the Old Testament, such as Noah and the Great Flood, are fiction developed to teach readers a particular spiritual truth. Despite the differences in interpretation, both schools believe that the words of the Bible were authored by God but penned by his chosen servants. Neither school continues to add material to the Bible, under the belief that Spirit is no longer inspiring writers the way she did in ancient times. It's as if a window to heaven was open for only a limited period of time, and in our era it is shut tight.

Given these beliefs, it's not surprising that some people shrink from the concept of writing their own scripture. A few of my clients have even thought the concept to be heretical or blasphemous. Given the heavy weight of infallibility and perfection, it's not surprising that the idea of writing scripture collapses under the pressure. However, it's critical to note that the definition of the word "scripture" was not always so rigid and narrow.

Although the contemporary definition of scripture may include the concepts of law and prophecy, its original meaning was simply "inspired by God." Gerhard Kittel and Gerhard Friedrich's *Greek Theological Dictionary of the New Testament* states that it was not until centuries after the Bible was written that the term came to have a legal, authoritative, or scholastic meaning. During the time when most of what we in the Western world commonly refer to as scripture was written, it was seen as no more sacred than what you or I might compose at our computer keyboard.

I choose to follow the original definition of the word rather than the one that has developed and predominates now. Given that, it is possible for any of us to engage in this kind of writing. It is a myth to think that Spirit is less available to you than he was to the authors of any of the world's sacred texts. He loves you no less or more than them; consequently, he is equally willing to offer you Spirit inspiration and wisdom. You can write psalms as beautiful as those written by King David or poems as powerful as those authored by Lao Tzu in the Tao Te Ching, and their ability to carry timeless wisdom will be just as powerful. For example, I wrote an essay on lessons learned from struggle that could just as easily apply in today's culture or many years into the future:

> *Times of crisis are often the greatest catalysts for our digging deeper channels for the root web of our faith to expand. While we don't welcome difficult times, God can use them to help us grow into a*

mighty oak tree. If I had to live my life over again I wouldn't choose ill health or divorce, but because of my response to those experiences I am at a place in my spiritual life where the view is incredible! I can see for miles and miles. In this place, I realize God and I are limitless.

You need not see visions or have doves descend upon you. There is no requirement that you be suitable for sainthood. Spirit doesn't play favorites. Everything you need is yours for the asking and receiving. If you make yourself available to receiving wisdom, it will be made available to you. Contrary to what some may believe, this is not inconsistent with the original biblical message. In the New Testament the Apostle Paul writes, "Let this mind be in you that was in Christ Jesus, who, being in the form of God, who, being One with God, thought it not robbery to stand equal with God" (Philippians 2:5).

This definition of scripture encompasses Huston Smith's definition of sacred art. Not only will Spirit inspire what you write, but it also will create a triangular relationship among you, the Spirit, and any reader of your text. Meeting this definition will be, though, the end of the limitations placed on the work. Within the framework of this definition you have complete freedom. Whatever you choose to write—as long as it carries Spirit's truth and establishes a window through which you and Spirit can be seen by the reader—will fall into the category of scriptural writing. However you capture that wisdom, whether through poetry or fiction or music, is up to you. As with every other part of the creation process, the fact that this is *your* personal sacred text means that the only judge of what should or should not be included is you.

You Can Write Scripture

ONCE YOU DECIDE that writing scripture is something you want to do, you may still have to jump the hurdle of believing it is something you *can* do. Most of us begin our lives as very creative and expressive people. We finger paint, build huge forts out of cardboard boxes, and make up bedtime stories to scare and amaze all our friends. But beginning in school, when grading and criticism become a regular part of our lives, we may find that the free-spirited creativity gradually was replaced with the certainty and seriousness of science, math, and grammatical sentence structure. By the time we reach adulthood, the majority of our world is dominated by linear, analytical thinking. Expression through art and writing has become something to be feared rather than enjoyed.

It is important to remember, though, that even if you haven't written a story or composed a poem for decades—or perhaps you never have—your capacity to do so has not disappeared. We are a creative species of being. Our right brain is dedicated to nonlinear intuitive thought patterns. Just because our culture favors and rewards rational behavior over artistic expression does not mean that our ability to write poetry has died an evolutionary death. Rest assured, you still have all of the creative capacities you were born with. You will simply need to begin exercising them again in order to build up your skill.

One of the greatest gifts you can give yourself in this process of writing your own scripture will be learning to silence your inner critic. That is the censor part of your thinking process, probably rooted in your left brain, that tells you things like "You can't write a story!" or "Remember the C Mrs. Gibbons gave your essay in the third grade?" or even "Why would you even bother to try writing your own scripture? Do you even know how to write a poem?" If you allow yourself to listen to this critical voice or, even worse, believe it, you will find the process of writing your own scripture both arduous and frustrating.

But how do you not listen? You can begin by turning the volume down for short periods of time. Say to yourself, "You might be right. But for the next ten minutes I'm going to try anyway." Don't argue with the critical message or try to defeat its power, just set it aside for small chunks of time. You always can go back and pick it up afterward. As you gain greater and greater practice and experience, you will find it easier to leave the critic for longer periods of time, and perhaps permanently.

During my workshops, I walk participants through a visualization exercise of separating themselves from their inner critic. They are guided to leave that censor in an enclosed room or faraway place while they pursue writing someplace else. While they're imagining themselves creating their scripture, I ask them to develop several positive affirmations that they can repeat to themselves instead of listening to the old destructive messages. Then when they finally do sit down, in reality, to write their scripture, they have two tools with which to address their inner critic: the ability to separate from the critic and the words to encourage rather than discourage the writing process.

You can enjoy these same benefits by following the steps in this exercise:

1. Take a few moments to relax, do some deep breathing, and consciously release the tension from your muscles.

2. Imagine, in your mind's eye, what your inner critic looks like. What is her physical appearance and demeanor? Try to be as detailed as possible. What is she wearing? How does she hold her body? What is the expression on her face?

3. See yourself escorting that inner critic to a large bank vault. It is a large room with a very sophisticated lock on the outside door.

4. Have the inner critic go inside the vault and shut the door behind her, turning the lock and securing it. If you like, set the lock to open automatically in a specified period of time.

5. Go to a place where you feel comfortable and at peace. Perhaps this is a room in your house or a natural setting. Imagine all of the details around you. Where will you sit? What is the temperature? What can you see around you?

6. Imagine before you a large, clean desk with all of the writing supplies you will need: pens, paper, your computer, and so on.

7. Feel yourself receiving energy from Spirit. Imagine your whole body filling with creative energy. What does it feel like? Do not allow any criticism or doubt to come into your mind—those belong to your inner critic, who is safely shut away from you.

8. With that energy arrives wisdom and inspiration from Spirit. You know instantly what you will write about, what format your writing will take, and how the words will flow together.

9. See yourself writing as long as you'd like, as much as you'd like. Feel your satisfaction at having captured everything you wanted to say exactly as you wanted to say it.

10. When you are finished, read what you wrote and enjoy the satisfaction of succeeding in your task.

Writing Resources

ANOTHER STUMBLING block to your confidence in writing your own scripture can be that you aren't sure what you'll write about or how you will put your truth into words. The following general references on writing can help you gain a greater understanding of this part of the process of creating your personal sacred text. Chapter 13 will provide you with specific writing tips in a variety of formats, from poetry, to essays, to fiction.

Spiritual Quests: The Art and Craft of Religious Writing, edited by William Zinsser
This book contains six chapters written by different authors detailing their experiences in writing work of a spiritual nature. The material was originally presented as a series of lectures at the New York Public Library in 1987. The authors are remarkably candid about their personal journeys and struggles with combining an abstract concept like spirituality with the concrete task of writing.

Writing from the Inner Self by Elaine Ferris Hughes
Hughes has created a writing process that incorporates meditation and visualization. She provides chapter after chapter of instruction and exercises on topics such as capturing emotions on paper and people watching as a source of inspiration.

Your Story Matters: Introducing the Pleasures of Personal Writing by Susan Paul
Paul has written a very simple introductory text to writing your spiritual story. She provides a detailed and beautiful description for why your writing is invaluable to the world, along with basic directions on journaling, poetry, prose, and letters.

Starting Points

ARE YOU STRUGGLING to begin the process of writing your own scripture because you don't have a subject to seek inspiration about? If so, try these suggestions for provoking ideas:

A turning point in my life
Sayings I've lived by
Inside I am . . .

How my beliefs have changed since I was young

I am ignorant of _____ and proud of it

When I am alone . . .

My earliest memory

Patterns in my life

Ways I didn't want to be, but I am

When I look in the mirror

A place where I always feel close to Spirit

The greatest lesson I have learned

My first encounter with Spirit

If I had to do _____ over again I would . . .

TWELVE

Methods of Seeking Inspiration to Write Your Own Scripture

W RITING YOUR OWN scripture is an exciting adventure. It takes you to places inside your heart and soul that you have never been. Your concept of Spirit expands into uncharted territories. The way you relate to others deepens to new levels.

While this is a wonderful thing, it requires trailblazing. When you selected materials written by others you were taking advantage of their completed creative-writing process. But in this part of your journey you must undertake that effort yourself. You will be the one to drill the well into the River of Truth and then try to capture your experience in words.

As you seek to make direct contact with Spirit, you may encounter everything from writer's block, to a lack of time to devote the energy you need to the process. Your progress will be slower and require much more of you than your earlier travels. You may tire and become frustrated. That is normal and to be expected. Take as many breaks for as long as you need to.

You may get so discouraged that you'll want to turn back altogether. When this happens, close the book, fold up your notes, and set the whole process aside for a while. Take a breath . . . a walk . . . a nap. Wait until that still, small voice inside you says it's time to try again. Never force yourself into making this part of the journey. If you do I promise you will not like the result. Your writing will lack authenticity, vitality, and depth. Instead, wait. When the moment is right you'll know.

I've outlined some methods to inspire you with your writing: guided visualization, journaling, Lectio Divina, meditation, and prayer. You may do just fine without these. But for those moments when you have questions but no answers, when you're not sure what you want to say, or when your creative expression seems at a dead end, these can be wonderful ways to tap into the wisdom and power of Spirit.

Some of the methods I discuss are ancient spiritual practices while others are more contemporary methods of self-discovery not typically associated with faith development. Although a few of them were developed within a specific religious orientation, in the form presented here they can be used regardless of your belief system. I chose a wide variety of methods that are easy to use and have many accessible resources.

For a general introduction to these methods I recommend two books to my clients. The first is Eileen Oster's *Healing Mind: Your Guide to the Power of Meditation, Prayer, and Reflection.* This is written from a mind/body perspective and also provides information on chakras and other life-energy sources. Marjorie Thompson's *Soul Feast: An Invitation to the Christian Spiritual Life* is written from a Christian perspective but is easily translatable to fit any spiritual tradition.

Spiritual Practice

BEFORE I DISCUSS each method individually, I want to elaborate on a theological issue about spiritual practice and its relationship to receiving inspiration from Spirit. Many faith communities believe that consistent, regimented use of one or more spiritual practices is required in order to build or maintain a relationship with Spirit. Some believers wear the frequency and amount of meditation or prayer they engage in each day like a badge of honor upon their chest. It's as if Spirit has a big chart for each of us where we get a star for each hour we've meditated, and when we earn enough of them we are rewarded with his approval and attention.

I've witnessed, and participated in, many discussions about this subject that were nothing more than spiritual pissing contests. I remember this specifically about my seminary days when we were required to take classes with ominous sounding names like Spiritual Discipline. Someone would inevitably report that she rose at five o'clock each morning to spend sixty minutes in prayer before she roused the kids, fixed breakfast, got dressed, and dashed out of the house to work. We would all "ooh" and "ahh" over this dedication to God and talk about how we wished we could do the same.

I always walked away from the discussions feeling like a peon in the spiritual hierarchy of life because I was not as devoted to my own prayer life. Those thoughts were a direct result of my belief in the popular myth that a prerequisite to relationship with Spirit was frequent and extensive engagement in an activity like prayer or meditation.

Now, years later and after much trial and experimentation, I realize how false that teaching is. The practice of a spiritual activity does not gain us worth or favor. It is not required to convince Spirit to attend to our needs. *There is no requirement for a faith relationship.* It is important to understand the messages behind the myth that there are requirements for a relationship with Spirit, namely that we are separate from Spirit and earn union with him only through the performance of specific behavior. If we buy into this myth, we are set up to feel alone and without value.

Nothing could be further from the truth. From the moment Spirit created you in your mother's womb, and perhaps even before, he has been with you. Even if you did not believe in or recognize a faith in any spiritual entity, he was there. The two of you are permanently intertwined, whether you choose to acknowledge that fact or not. Furthermore, your value and right to receive unconditional love is a given. It is not predicated on any beliefs, words, or actions that you espouse, speak, or do. Spirit loved you from the moment he created you. There is no way to earn that or lose it. You have value simply because you exist.

Although these concepts are not foreign to most Eastern philosophies, they are a radical, and perhaps even heretical, departure from most Western traditions. An integral part of most Christian teachings is the teaching that not only is God a separate entity, but that he does not join in relationship with you until you repent from your sins and invite him into your life.

During my first year in seminary I had an encounter with another student about this subject that remains vividly imprinted on my memory. I was paired with a classmate for the purpose of performing role-plays about working with drug-addicted clients. When it was her turn to take the part of the therapist, she began asking me questions about my faith in God, even though we were supposed to be discussing my problems attending Alcoholics Anonymous meetings. I finally became so frustrated I stopped and asked her why she was pursuing this line of questioning.

She replied that unless I, as the client, had been "born again," I would not be able to attain sobriety because only people "who had invited God into their hearts" were capable of doing good things. That response shocked me. Although well intentioned and not at all ignorant concerning theological matters, this woman honestly believed that only Christians had the ability to act out of love and kindness. This was possible not because of who they were but only because they had a relationship with God. All nonbelievers were consequently incapable of doing well because they were motivated purely by selfishness and greed.

Although I believed some variation of this same concept for most of my life, being presented with such an extreme view shook me. It was impossible to ignore the absurdity of her comment. At that moment I chose to abandon my belief that what I think or do is connected to my self-worth or relationship with Spirit. Doing so left a hole in my faith that I could not fill for a long time. Only when I began studying Eastern philosophies and religions did I find a more healthy replacement. I know that beliefs similar to this lie in many Western traditions too, but it was in Buddhism and Taoism that I found the answer for myself.

I am not saying that spiritual practices, especially those described in this chapter, are bad or without purpose. They have tremendous value, but only if you use them with a healthy understanding of their intention. Spiritual practices ground us, center us, and elevate us into a Spirit level of consciousness.

But their effect is upon us, not Spirit. No amount of prayer is going to result in him loving you more. You cannot meditate enough hours in the day to move Spirit closer to you. You can, though, become more aware of him through all of the methods presented in this chapter.

When you use the following methods in your quest to write your own scripture, do so with the understanding that they are neither necessary for nor a guarantee of receiving inspiration. They don't motivate Spirit to act. He is not manipulated by our behavior but by his love for us. Spirit is as available to you as much now as he would be if you never uttered a word in prayer for the rest of your life.

If you do choose to practice one of these tools, you will cultivate your receptivity to inspiration, creating fertile ground for ideas and topics to take root. Then, when Spirit has something she wants you to write about, you'll pick up even the faintest of signals. And if you've been regularly tuning into that higher frequency of Spirit-consciousness through any one of these practices, you will know quickly and with great clarity that the message is of Spirit.

But even if you choose not to pray, Spirit won't make you jump through hoops to find inspiration. She will still provide it. It may be a bit muddled at first, but she will keep talking until you receive it loud and clear.

Some of these methods are designed to be practiced for a specific period of time. For example, the Centering Prayer should be engaged in for twenty minutes daily. In using others, such as journaling, you may choose to set a time limit on your sessions. In these instances, keep a clock or watch nearby and check it occasionally. After a while, you will develop an intuitive sense for when the time has elapsed. If you elect to use some form of timer, set the volume on a very low setting. You do not want a sudden sound to jar you from your concentration.

Now that you know the purpose and some common guidelines for using these methods of seeking inspiration, let's take a close look at each one.

Guided Visualization

GUIDED VISUALIZATION (also referred to as guided imagery), like journaling, is typically known as a tool for self-discovery and freeing creativity. It is essentially a method of exploring using the mind rather than the body, expanding our thinking in ways that the limits of reality prevent. It is a great way to find inspiration. So we will take full advantage of it here.

The power behind this process rests in the way our neurological system is designed. When we imagine an experience by incorporating all five of our senses, our mind is tricked into thinking that it is actually occurring. Without having to worry about the constraints of time, money, or access, we can go anywhere and be limited only by our capacity to imagine the experience. For this reason it is important that you use guided visualization tapes or scripts that are as detailed as possible in their sensory information.

You can purchase tapes from your local bookseller or order a tape from the Whole Person Associates catalog listed on page 176. To help you write your own scripture, I have written two scripts tailored to the process of creating a personal sacred text. They can be used when you are alone or with your journey partner or group. As it is impossible to immerse yourself in the visualization process while reading from a book, you will want to record them by reading them into a tape recorder.

The scripts provide multiple opportunities to customize the visualization. You will be asked to specify elements of the environment, your own experience with it, and, most important, the wisdom that you seek and receive. When a question is asked, don't force an answer. Know that somewhere inside you lies the information. Pause as long as necessary. Let it rise in its own time. This whole experience is about tapping into your own intuitive knowledge and your direct channel to Spirit. Move on when you have a clear visualization of the requested element.

SCRIPT ONE: A WALK IN THE FOREST

As you settle into a comfortable position, gently close your eyes. Begin to slow your breathing into a rhythmic pattern of cycling air into and out of your lungs. They don't need to be especially deep breaths. Focus instead on making them unhurried and effortless. Start to clear your mind of the day's clutter. Bring yourself completely into the present moment. Check in with every part of your body. Where are you feeling tension? Take a few moments to relax muscles that are tense or release worries that you are holding. Let your body and mind become lighter and calmer with each breath.

When you are ready, begin to form a forest in your mind's eye. Picture the evergreen trees, their trunks covered with moss, reaching into the sky until you cannot see their tops. Are there clouds up there or is it clear? Perhaps it's overcast and there is a fog settling like a gray curtain over the tree branches.

Look around at eye level now. What do you see? Are there birds in the trees? Picture them in detail. What kind are they? What color are they? Are they singing? Take a moment and listen to their song.

Look down. See the dirt covered in pine needles, the rocks, and the lush green ferns growing amid the trees. Is the ground dry or damp? Take a moment and breathe in the earthy smell of the soil. As you immerse yourself in the sights, sounds, and scents of the forest, you feel completely safe and at peace.

What is the weather like today? Can you feel the heat or the cold on your skin? Is there a mist in the air that collects on your face? Take a moment to imagine what you would be wearing given those weather conditions. See yourself in the clothes you would choose for your walk in the forest. Touch your coat or shirt sleeves, feel your feet on the ground, and brush a pine needle from your leg.

In front of you there is a dirt path into the forest. It is about three feet wide and cleared of any rocks, tree limbs, or plants that would impede your travel. Stepping forward onto the path, you hear the ground crunch beneath your feet. As you walk along the path you reach out and touch a tree. Feel the rough bark under your finger. A bird darts by, barely missing you on its way to joining others that have settled onto a nearby branch. You listen to their song fade behind you as you travel farther into the forest. Note other animals that you encounter or insects that fly by. Take a deep breath through your mouth and feel the crisp forest air flow over your tongue, down your throat, and into your lungs. Focus on the details of what you see, hear, smell, touch, and taste in the environment around you. Feel your sense of calm and relaxation deepen as you progress along the path.

After you have walked for a distance, you see a clearing in the forest before you. As you get closer to it you can see people seated on the ground. Their backs are to you so you can't quite tell what they are doing. Then, above the noise of the birds and the tree branches rustling together, you hear a voice telling a story about someone making a voyage. Take a moment and imagine what the voice sounds like. Is it male or female? Is it strong or gentle, authoritative or light? Is it spoken with a rhythm or is there a clear, steady intonation?

With every footfall you come closer to the edge of the clearing. Now you can clearly see a cluster of people sitting on the ground intently focused on the storyteller. Study them for a moment. How are they dressed? How old are they? What is their gender? How many people are seated there?

As you continue to walk into the clearing, the speaker is beginning to come into view. Shift your attention to that person. They are moving easily in front of the group, gesturing as they tell their story. There is a very relaxed and unhurried air about them. Instantly, you have an intuitive knowledge that this is a very wise storyteller, someone who has the answers to questions you have asked for years. What do they look like? How are they dressed? What is their age? How are their feet, legs, arms, and hands moving? As you study this person, they turn their gaze from the seated audience to you. Your eyes meet.

"Hello," the storyteller says, "I'm so glad to see you. We've been waiting for you." They beckon you forward with their hand. "Come, join us. There is a place for you right here."

The people seated on the ground turn to you and smile. They move to either side and form a pathway through their midst. You walk forward. The storyteller points to a place in the direct center of everyone, left open just for you. As you lower yourself to the ground, feel the dirt under your hands and the earth supporting your weight. Several of those seated welcome you with brief greetings. One says, "Hello" and another, "It's good to see you." Others simply nod. In that place and moment you feel unconditionally accepted and loved by everyone present.

The speaker continues the story. "And the travelers finally arrived in the circle of wisdom. There they are welcomed. All of the answers they seek are here for them to find. They need only ask." The storyteller turns to face you directly, looking straight into your eyes. "What do you need to know?"

You pause. You have never been asked this question so pointedly. Yet intuitively you know that this storyteller possesses all the world's ancient and contemporary wisdom. Their promise to address your concern is not empty. They have a connection to Spirit that will enable them to give you any answer. Knowing this, a question rises into your consciousness—something that's been on your mind for a while. What is it that you have to ask today? Take a few moments to formulate your wording and then ask the storyteller your questions.

They briefly pause. "That is indeed a concern worthy of attention.

Let me tell you how Spirit will provide you with the wisdom you are seeking." Without additional hesitation the storyteller begins to speak to the entire group, eloquently addressing your question. What form does the answer take? A poem? A story? An essay? Is it lengthy or brief? Hear the words as you watch the speaker's lips form them. You won't need to remember them exactly because they are being stored effortlessly in your memory. Instead, savor hearing the response and making it your own, for it was formulated specifically with you in mind.

When the speaker is finished, thank him or her. Thank the people around you for welcoming you to their circle. As you stand, they move aside and allow you to walk back through the clearing to the path. With every step you become less aware of the forest and more aware of your body in this present moment. Refocus on your breathing. Feel the chair or ground beneath you and your body resting on it. Slowly open your eyes. When you're ready, write down the wisdom that the storyteller gave you. However you remember it is exactly how it should be recalled. Use it in the days to come to write your scriptures.

SCRIPT TWO: GIFTS FROM THE OCEAN

As you settle into a comfortable position, gently close your eyes. Begin to slow your breathing into a rhythmic pattern of cycling air into and out of your lungs. They don't need to be especially deep breaths. Focus instead on making them unhurried and effortless. Start to clear your mind of the day's clutter. Bring yourself completely into the present moment. Check in with every part of your body. Where are you feeling tension? Take a few moments to relax muscles that are tense or release worries that you are holding. Let your body and mind become lighter and calmer with each breath.

When you are ready, begin to imagine yourself standing on a beach. Look up and down the coastline, noting the cliffs, rock formations, and sand dunes. Is this a site you are familiar with, or is it someplace you have never visited? Is there driftwood on the beach? Are there shells, seaweed, or tide pools? Look out to the horizon. Watch the waves roll in and out.

It is a mild, sunny day. Feel the warmth of the sun upon your face. What are you wearing? Observe your clothing and how it feels on your body. Smell the salt and sea air. The wind blows across your body. Can you feel mist pelting your face? Is there sand in the breeze? Can you taste the salt that it carries?

Begin to walk down the beach, along the edge of the water where the sand turns firm and hard. Feel your feet sink a little bit with each step. Observe the footprints that trail behind you. Your stride is leisurely. You are enjoying the peaceful walk.

Something in front of you catches your eye. Just beyond the tide's reach is a book lying in the sand. It must, you imagine, have been washed ashore by the waves. As you get closer to it you can see that it is still in good shape despite its seagoing voyage. What does it look like? Note its color, size, and thickness. Stop beside it and kneel down in the sand. There is a title printed on the cover and along the spine. It reads *Truth and Wisdom*. There is no author's name or other illustration.

Reach down and touch the book. Feel its wet and cold cover. There is sand crusted over portions of the spine; it feels rough under your fingers as you brush it off. Open the cover to read the initial page. You are amazed that although the page is wet, it is not damaged. You can clearly read what is written on it:

To all who may find this book:

Transcribed on these pages is the wisdom of the entire universe. Answers to life's most perplexing problems, troubles, and challenges are recorded here as well as all of the guidance and intelligence that has ever existed. There is no truth that is not contained between the covers of this book. It is yours for the taking and receiving, a gift freely given by the Spirit that loves you.

After finishing this page, you turn it to find a detailed table of contents. As your finger scans the subject listing, a question or concern begins to form in your mind. There is something you had been searching for, a piece of wisdom or truth that has evaded your knowledge and expression up to this point. Just as you reach a final determination of the subject you are specifically seeking, you move your finger down to see it appear in black-and-white lettering. As you look over to your right, you see a page number referenced.

You can feel your anticipation rising as you thumb through the book until you locate the correct page number. Dividing the pages in that place you can see the heading you were seeking. Beneath it is paragraph after paragraph of information that is perfectly suited to your concern. As you read through the words, you are astonished at the wisdom and truth that they contain. Intuitively you realize that this exactly what you need to know. Read through each sentence, paragraph, and page carefully. Don't worry about committing the information exactly to memory. Trust that you will remember what you need to exactly as you need to. Instead, focus on the essence of the message and on understanding how it applies to your life.

When you are finished close the book. Although you could take it with you, you choose to leave it there for others to enjoy. After all, you can always come back to it yourself if the need arises. Stand up and turn to head back in the direction you came. Feel the sun, mist, and wind on your face and body. Look out into the sea of water and expanse of sky above and say a quick thank you to the Universe for providing you the wisdom you sought.

With every step you become less aware of the beach and more aware of your body in this present moment. Refocus on your breathing. Feel the chair or ground beneath you and your body resting on it. Slowly open your eyes. When you're ready, write down the wisdom that the book gave you. However you remember it is exactly how it should be recalled. Use it in the days to come to write your scripture.

HOW TO USE GUIDED VISUALIZATION

ALTHOUGH COMPLEX in the way it involves all levels of our mind, body, and soul, the process of guided visualization is actually quite simple. Once you have your guided visualization tape—either one you have purchased or one you have made—follow these steps to use it:

1. Take your tape recorder to a place where you can sit or lie down comfortably without distraction. The visualizations I have written will take about ten minutes; others will vary but the length should be clearly stated on the cassette or compact disc.

2. Before you turn the recording on, take a few deep breaths, clear your mind, and relax your body.

3. Start the tape or disc and focus completely on the instructions. They will take you step by step through an imaginary process of exploring a particular place and/or activity.

4. It is of particular importance that you engage all of your senses. For each sight, sound, smell, taste, and touch presented, silently ask yourself questions: How blue is the sky? Do you recognize the odor of wet earth or wildflowers as you walk along? Can you taste the salt from the sea air blowing onto your face? What is the temperature of the water flowing at your feet? How does it feel running over your fingers?

5. At the conclusion of the visualization, the tape will guide you through a short process of reorienting to the present time and place.

6. Keep your journal or notebook close by to record your experience afterward.

A note of caution about using the guided visualization process: Kinesthetic stimuli can be powerful triggers of memories. Be aware of this and stop the process if something unpleasant arises for you. If you are a survivor of some form of trauma, as a child or an adult, you may want to discuss using this process with your therapist or a trusted friend. At the very least, develop a safety plan for what you will do if something painful or upsetting comes up.

HERE ARE SOME RESOURCES for further instruction on guided visualization:

> Whole Person Associates (210 West Michigan, Duluth, Minnesota 55802-1908/800-247-6789) offers a wide variety of audio- and videotapes for relaxation and guided visualization by mail order. Their materials are not limited to creative or spiritual discovery and cover an amazing variety of topics. Of particular interest for your purpose are the audiocassettes entitled *Spiritual Centering*, *Personal Empowering*, *Refreshing Journeys*, and *Healing Vision*. They are of different lengths, typically from five to twenty minutes.

> *Creative Visualization* by Shakti Gawain
> This is the best book on the use of guided visualization for energizing the creative process. It is written in a workbook format with step-by-step guidance and space to complete exercises. Companion audio- and videotaped visualizations are also available.

Journaling

YOU PROBABLY HAVE already heard a lot about the process of keeping a journal. It has become wildly popular in every segment of the population, especially in the last decade. More than 5 million journals are sold in the United States every year. If you're like me you have six or seven of them, all in various stages of completion, tucked away in various locations around the house.

This is the one method of seeking inspiration presented in this chapter least associated with spiritual development. It is traditionally perceived as a tool for record keeping, expressing creativity, and promoting self-awareness and personal growth. I propose you continue to use your journal for all of these reasons, but now you can begin to focus on how it can interact with your spirituality.

The process of journaling can be simple or complex. In its most basic form it consists of jotting down an idea or two in a spiral-bound notebook once or twice a week. On the other end of the spectrum is the bound volume that is faithfully used every day to record lengthy descriptions of events, feelings, goals, and philosophies.

Most of your efforts will fall somewhere in between, varying somewhat according to the events and changes in your life. This is a reflection of the great beauty of journaling. There are no hard-and-fast rules. It is a very individual and dynamic practice.

If you're just beginning a journal, I suggest you start small. Too many people have begun an elaborate program, only to give the whole process up within a short time because it proved too difficult to maintain. Build a plan around the following basic questions.

What are you going to write in?
It's okay to use an ordinary pad of paper, or you can invest in one of the blank books that are widely available in most drug, discount, and bookstores.

How often will you write?
"Once a week" or "whenever I feel moved" are both good answers. If you're going to set an initial goal of writing daily, set a limit on how much you'll write. Don't be hard on yourself if you miss a day; otherwise you'll set yourself up to fail.

When and where will you write?

Choose a time and place where you will have some privacy. It's hard to be absorbed in the process with a screaming toddler clasped to your ankle, not to mention how your child will feel. It may help to aim for the same time each day in order to get yourself into the habit.

How much will you write?

Starting small is essential. Try setting a time or length limit, such as ten minutes or ten sentences. Some days you might do more, some less. Again, the idea is to establish a successful beginning. As you progress you can increase the amount or drop the limit altogether.

What will you write about?

Starting with a more factual account of daily events or goals is a safe and nonthreatening way to settle into the journaling process. Pouring out your heart may be overwhelming or even unfamiliar to you in the beginning. That's okay. Start where you are with what feels right and gradually move yourself into a more challenging and consciousness-expanding subject.

Topics to consider that I believe will facilitate scripture writing are childhood lessons and beliefs; suffering; how to live what you believe; love of self, Spirit, and others; dreams and visions for the future; turning points; perspective; attitude; choice; conscious living; service; and starting over.

What style will your entries follow?

You could try letters, dialogues, poems, diatribes, lectures, jokes, and prayers. You could write in complete sentences, phrases, bulleted lists and thoughts, or streams of consciousness with no breaks or punctuation at all. Try a variety of formats before you settle on one. You may find yourself switching around depending on your mood and the subject matter.

The goal of journaling for your purpose is to create a heightened awareness of yourself and your relationship with Spirit. As you track your increasing self-awareness or the development of concepts about who Spirit is and how you interact with him, patterns and themes will float to the surface. These will be the seeds that grow into your scripture writing.

An example from my journaling process is the theme of grief and loss. Because I had experienced so much of it in my life, I found myself returning to it again and again. I was trying to understand why I was having such a hard time "getting over" my painful experiences. After years of grappling with the issue, I wrote:

There is a point where grief is so overwhelming that it becomes numbing, and you cease to feel. Then things don't seem to matter anymore. Things that were important fade away, and get left undone or avoided. Life ceases to be worthwhile. The grief takes on a life of its own, actually becomes a dynamic force. All of your self disappears in the face of an emotion that settles deep inside, and like an acid, eats you from the inside out. The most important things go first, like your will to live, faith, self-esteem, and identity. Now you are grief. You have faith in it because you know it will always be there. It will never betray your trust. You depend on it, and sometimes you even feed it because without it you would be empty. It's eaten everything else away and you can't remember what used to be there before the grief came and took it all away.

Several years later I used this entry as the inspiration for a poem I added to my sacred text about the gifts of wisdom I received from my experiences of grief. You will want to review your journal periodically to search for similar patterns and themes. Take a highlighter and mark entries that you think are important and could be instrumental in your scripture writing.

. . .

HERE ARE RESOURCES for further instruction on journaling:

At a Journal Workshop: Writing to Access the Power of the Unconscious and Evoke Creative Ability by Ira Progoff
This classic book describes Progoff's detailed journaling process. If you love journaling and want to create a volume for cataloging everything from your dreams to inner dialogue, this is the book for you!

Life's Companion: Journal Writing as a Spiritual Quest by Christina Baldwin
This is one of the few books that view journaling as a way to track your spiritual journey. It has exercises and ideas for your own writing as well as examples from the author and participants from her workshops.

Notes from Myself: A Guide to Creative Journal Writing by Anne Hazard Aldrich
This resource focuses on recording the process of self-discovery and development through journaling. It contains a wealth of guidance, ideas, and exercises.

Lectio Divina

ALTHOUGH PROBABLY the least well known of the spiritual practices listed in this chapter, Lectio Divina, Latin for "Spirit reading," is the one I would most highly recommend for personal scripture writing. It is essentially a method of studying scriptural material to obtain personal insight. It is my favorite because it is easy to practice but results in the realization of amazing wisdom. If you like variety, this is the method for you because it combines reading, contemplation, meditation, and prayer.

Lectio Divina is also more action oriented than some of the other methods described. Thinking is not only encouraged, it's necessary. If you have a hard time quieting your mind during meditative exercises, Lectio Divina may be a more suitable choice for you.

Lectio Divina was used exclusively within the Judeo-Christian tradition for centuries. Only within the last decade has it been slowly incorporated into the repertoire of spiritual practices of people from other faith backgrounds. It can be traced back to writings from the Old Testament, particularly in the Psalms. However, the process itself was not formalized and widely taught until promoted by Saint Benedict in the sixth century A.D.

The process of Lectio Divina begins with the selection of a reading that you wish to study in depth. Although originally intended to be used with overtly religious material, you may use the process with any type of writing you like. Choose a piece with a message, subject, setting, or philosophy that is currently resonating within you. Focus on a short selection, one to five pages long, especially if you only have a limited amount of time. I have used sacred texts, song lyrics, devotionals, and poetry, all with great success.

There are four parts to the Lectio Divina: lectio (reading), meditatio (meditation), oratio (prayer), and contemplatio (contemplation). The whole process usually takes at least twenty minutes and can last for hours depending on the text you use.

1. Find a comfortable spot that will afford you complete privacy for the length of your study and reflection.

2. Take a few deep breaths, clear your mind, and ground your spirit by focusing inward rather than on the external world.

3. When you're ready, move into the first stage of lectio, or reading. Work slowly and gently through your text, savoring each word. You can read aloud or silently, whichever you find more pleasing. If you've read this passage before, pretend you haven't.

4. Question the meaning of each sentence and phrase for you personally at this moment in your life. Repeatedly ask Spirit, aloud or silently, "What message do you have for me in this word/sentence/passage?"

5. When a particular word or phrase catches in your heart, stop reading and move on to the next step of meditatio.

6. Meditatio, or meditation, involves searching for the meaning behind the word, phrase, or concept that has caught your attention. The question to ask Spirit during this segment is "What do you want me to do with this message?" Using the example of a phrase about forgiveness, the answer could be as simple as "Don't forget this line, you'll need it soon," or as involved as "You need to resolve your conflict with Mom."

7. After you have some sense of what Spirit wants you to do with the message you've received, continue with oratio.

8. Oratio, or prayer, offers a time to respond to and interact with Spirit about what you've learned in the lectio and meditatio stages. Perhaps they have evoked anger or gratitude in you. Share that with Spirit. Seek further clarification or more specifics about how to carry out the message. Weep if the message has brought release, pain, or joy.

9. If you still have time and want to continue, return to lectio and continue reading where you left off. You can repeat this cycle as many times as you wish.

10. When you have completed as many cycles of the first three stages as you wish, it is time to move on to contemplatio.

11. Contemplatio, or contemplation, is a time of rest, of clearing the mind, of centering and preparing to reenter your daily life. Take as much time as you need, but at least five minutes, to complete this stage.

12. After you have completed Lectio Divina, take a few minutes to write down the messages you received. I have a section in my journal titled "Lectio Divina Wisdom." Some of my best scripture writing has had its start there.

HERE ARE RESOURCES for further instruction on Lectio Divina:

Lectio Divina by Basil Pennington
Pennington is an expert on a variety of spiritual practices that are rooted in the Christian tradition. This is a well-researched and comprehensive guidebook on Lectio Divina.

Sacred Reading: The Ancient Art of Lectio Divina by Michael Casey
This is a bestselling book in the United States about the process of Lectio Divina.

Too Deep for Words: Rediscovering Lectio Divina by Thelma Hall
This is a good introductory text. It is written in simple terms using a very commonsense approach, avoiding a lot of the theological language you'll find in other books about spiritual subjects. The short length (128 pages) also makes it an attractive choice for you if you are short on time or want more information quickly.

http://www.ptw.com/~standrab/ld-art.html
This website built by Father Luke Dysinger and St. Andrew's Abbey has good information on Lectio Divina that includes guided studies for individuals and groups.

Meditation

ONCE PRACTICED only by flower children and members of religious groups rooted in Eastern tradition, meditation has now crossed over into both Western spiritual traditions and mainstream secular culture. Although it is used in a variety of settings—from birthing classes to dental offices—as a simple tool to reduce stress and induce relaxation, it has the potential to do much more than that. Many Westerners also misunderstand the goal of meditation, thinking it is to empty the mind or consciousness. Actually meditation is a process of transcending the mind and uniting with a higher level of consciousness. It is this end result that makes it such a wonderful tool for receiving inspiration from Spirit to write your scripture.

There are two primary meditation techniques: transcendental and vipassana. The former originates from a pre-Hindu philosophy and the latter from the Buddhist tradition. While they are similar in methodology, their purpose is significantly different.

TRANSCENDENTAL MEDITATION

THE PRACTICE OF transcendental meditation has its origins in the pre-Hindu Vedic movement of approximately 1500 to 1400 B.C. Followers of this movement thought that every man possessed a higher level of consciousness that represents his truest self, an idea that is now one of the major tenets of the Hindu faith. If followers realized this level of consciousness, accessed it, and maintained it, they believed they would be free from suffering and attain a state of *ananda,* or bliss.

Maharishi Mahesh Yogi developed the process of transcendental meditation in the early 1950s as a means of reaching this higher level of consciousness. He believed that in this state we connect with a field of pure creative intelligence from which all thought and action originate.

In 1955 he began teaching the method to others in India. Since that time it has become adopted throughout the world. With 1.5 million practitioners in the United States, it is easily the most widely used form of meditation in this country.

Transcendental meditation uses rhythmic breathing and the repetition of a mantra to facilitate relaxation and subsequent ascension into the higher level of consciousness. A mantra is a Sanskrit word that you choose or is chosen for you by your meditation teacher because it has particular symbolic meaning to you. Since my familiarity with Sanskrit doesn't begin to approach a sophisticated level, I will ask you to use the word "om" as your mantra. Even though it is not personalized, it is still a powerful choice. Research has shown that repetition of words ending in the letter n or m has a direct impact on our neurological system, causing increased relaxation and calmness.

The purpose of transcendental meditation is to reach your state of true being or higher level of consciousness and then capture the bliss you experience to bring back into your daily existence. It is recommended that you meditate twice a day for twenty minutes at a time, thus providing a steady stream of bliss to enter your life. More than 500 research studies have been conducted on the process and benefits of transcendental meditation. Their results support the claim that it improves physical, emotional, and mental health.

Such promising benefits are hard to resist. If you would like to try transcendental meditation, follow this process:

1. Again, find a time and place when you are least likely to be interrupted.

2. Sit on the floor using your best posture and find a position that will be comfortable for twenty minutes.

3. Close your eyes and quiet your body with several rounds of deep breathing.

4. Begin to repeat your mantra aloud in a slow, steady, rhythmic way.

5. Allow your entire focus to rest in the repetition of your mantra. It should be a gentle rather than forced process of increasing concentration.

6. As your neurological system slows down, you will likely experience a physical sensation experienced practitioners associate with the disconnecting of consciousness from the body.

7. Relax into the process and enjoy the experience of being in complete union with your highest self.

8. When time has elapsed, allow yourself a few moments to reorient. This is particularly important with transcendental meditation because it actually alters our body's processes, such as heart rate and blood pressure.

9. As with the other practices, don't rush off without capturing what you experience in a few written notes. You have just tapped into pure creativity. It would be a shame to dash off without taking full advantage of it.

HERE ARE RESOURCES for further instruction on transcendental meditation:

Happiness: The TM Program, Psychiatry, and Enlightenment by Harold Bloomfield
This is the longest enduring and most classic manual on transcendental meditation. While the scientific elements are now

a bit dated, the instruction is timeless, thorough, and understandable.

Science of Being and Art of Loving: Transcendental Meditation by
Maharishi Mahesh Yogi
You can't go wrong by going straight to the man who developed the technique.

Transcendental Meditation by Robert Roth
This is a very comprehensive book that stays true to the program developed by Maharishi Mahesh Yogi. It presents the method and scientific research that supports transcendental meditation's use, as well as interviews with practitioners from all walks of life. While I'm not sure that reading celebrity interviews will increase your effective use of this method, it does make for a fascinating and entertaining reading experience.

THE MAHARISHI Vedic Education Development Corporation maintains an extensive and informative United States Transcendental Meditation website at http://www.tm.org.

It provides scientific studies that validate the benefits of transcendental meditation, offers books and videos, and can refer you to a teaching center near you.

VIPASSANA MEDITATION

VIPASSANA IS A Sanskrit word with a complicated translation. Essentially, it means an intuitive awareness that all physical and mental phenomena are not real. They are, instead, only temporary constructions and reflections of our ego.

The definition becomes easier to understand when you know that Buddhists believe that nothing we encounter in this world is real, but is only a creation of our minds. In fact, they would not even acknowledge there is a world to begin with. Suffering is a result of our ego's interpretation of the kinesthetic information our mind and body receive. Active intention, rather than passive reaction, becomes critical. For example, hearing our boss say "You're fired" results in distress only because we give the sounds our ears hear meaning and power by associating them with something bad or unwanted. Understanding this principle means you can shift your perspective on life, intend to have a more accurate experience, end your suffering, and reach a state of nirvana, or bliss.

Vipassana meditation is somewhat paradoxical. It focuses on becoming acutely aware of mental and bodily processes so that you can become free of them, thereby avoiding suffering and reaching a state of nirvana. Diana St. Ruth captures the essence of the practice in her book *Sitting*:

> *Let the body experience itself. This is the way to be liberated from the body. . . . To be with the body completely is to be free of it totally. The same is true of the world and the mind. Awareness both in daily life and in formal sitting meditation brings this realization.*

Vipassana meditation emphasizes being fully present and aware in every moment and thus enables us to engage in life more fully with the intention of having a positive experience. If this sounds like something you would like to achieve, then try this process:

1. Find a time and place where you will be free from disruption. Initially you will be meditating for about ten minutes, increasing over time to thirty minutes.

2. Sit on the floor or in a chair with your spine erect and eyes closed.

3. Begin by taking slow, regular breaths. Focus on your breath in order to quiet your mind.

4. After your internal chatter has quieted down, turn your attention to the sensations in your body.

5. Note silently to yourself what you perceive, without judgment or interpretation. Your inner dialogue will sound something like: breathing . . . listening . . . aching in my right shoulder . . . breathing . . .

6. If your mind wanders from its course, note this as well, then return to your focus on becoming aware of what is going on in your body. Observe and be fully present with your body. As this happens you will find yourself becoming increasingly relaxed and at peace.

7. When your allotted time has ended allow yourself a few minutes to return to the present very gently. Slowly become increasingly aware of your body, mind, and surroundings.

8. Take a moment to write some notes about your experience before you return to your daily activities.

HERE ARE RESOURCES for further instruction on Vipassana meditation:

The Art of Living: Vipassana Meditation as Taught by S. N. Goenka by William Hart
The most comprehensive work on the market about this subject, as taught by a world-renowned expert in the field.

Purifying the Heart: Buddhist Insight Meditation for Christians by Kevin Culligan, Mary Jo Meadow, and Daniel Chowning
This is an excellent introduction to a Buddhist technique from a Christian perspective. The authors do a wonderful job

of integrating the teachings of both traditions that support the benefits of Vipassana meditation. This is the perfect book for readers approaching this technique from a Christian point of view.

Sitting: A Guide to Buddhist Meditation by Diana St. Ruth
Only seventy-eight pages, some illustrated, this is a basic introduction to Vipassana meditation for beginners.

The followers of S. N. Goenka, the leading expert in Vipassana meditation, maintain the best website on this method of seeking inspiration: http://www.dhamma.org. Aside from information on the history of the method and instructions on how to practice it yourself, they can refer you to ten-day Vipassana retreats being held in your area.

HERE ARE RESOURCES for further instruction on general meditative techniques:

The Best Guide to Meditation by Victor N. Davich
This is a contemporary meditation manual with instructions for the beginning, intermediate, and advanced student. It also provides different techniques depending on whether your goals are therapeutic or spiritual.

Learn to Meditate Kit by Patricia Carrington
This is a perfect choice for those of you who struggle to master the technique while flipping back and forth between a manual and meditation. Its four sixty-minute audiotapes, accompanied by that pesky manual, walk you through a variety of exercises and instructions.

Prayer

PRAYER IS THE most widely used spiritual practice in the world. Virtually every faith tradition teaches it in one form or another. Visit a church, temple, or mosque in any corner of the world and you will find congregants gathered in communal or individual prayer. It is one of the few universally practiced activities that cut across culture, age, gender, race, and socioeconomic status.

I think it is also the most misunderstood and overcomplicated spiritual practice, especially in the Western world. The purpose of prayer is to commune with Spirit. It's that simple. For a variety of reasons, most well-intentioned but some self-serving prayer is often contorted into what I describe as "begging, bragging, and disengaging." Spirit is not a heavenly Santa Claus. When we approach her for the main purpose of presenting a litany of requests, we do not accomplish our intended goal of interacting with her.

Yes, sharing our needs and wishes with Spirit is a part of prayer. But it is only one element of it, just as asking for things from our partners is one aspect our relationship with them. Can you imagine how our connections with our partners would not only stop developing but also start deteriorating if the only reason we sought them out was to read off a list of demands? No one would tolerate that for any length of time, yet we commonly ask Spirit to accept this limited type of relationship with us. When that's the case, we succeed only in cheating ourselves and stunting our spiritual growth.

Prayer is not intended to be used for the purpose of bragging either. As I stated earlier in this chapter, some people are eager to tell others how often and how long they pray because they have bought into the idea that engaging in spiritual practice is a measure of their worth. These people have really missed the point, as well as the benefits, of prayer.

But so do those who use prayer as a way to build themselves up.

Have you ever had lunch with someone who couldn't stop talking about himself and all the wonderful things he was doing? It makes for a very unbalanced and frustrating experience, not to mention a shallow one. When you sit down to talk to Spirit, make sure the conversation flows in both directions about a variety of issues.

When prayer is too rote or rigid, it becomes a way of disengaging from rather than interacting with Spirit. As a child in Catholic school I memorized prayers, creeds, catechisms, and rituals until you could look into my eyes and read them etched onto my brain. I learned to read using the Baltimore Catechism, Nicene Creed, Stations of the Cross, and portions of the Sunday Mass. All of them have an eloquent message and appropriate place in spiritual practice, but their overuse makes you nothing more than a robot going through the motions. When my mouth opened to recite them my mind darted off onto other topics, no matter how piously I tried to concentrate.

I think that the passage in the Bible containing the Lord's Prayer is one of the most misinterpreted. When Jesus said "Pray in this way," he did not mean "Memorize my specific words and repeat them for centuries to come." Instead he intended to show us a model for authentic and heartfelt communication with Spirit.

I'm sure that Spirit loves hearing recited prayers, just as most of us melt when our lover reads romantic poetry to us. But if that's all she does, we begin to wonder what happened to her own voice. God wants to know what we have to say, not just what others thought we should say.

Practicing a rigid prayer routine is also a way of disengaging our true selves from the process. From my early schooling until my final years in seminary I was presented with countless methods for speaking to Spirit. Each process outlined a series of specific steps to follow each time I prayed, detailing such things as when is the appropriate moment to confess my sins in prayer and exactly how to do that. When a rigid pattern is used, the focus of prayer becomes engaging with and adhering to that pattern rather than Spirit. If talking to someone you love is so hard that you need a rigid, preset process to get you through it, there's something wrong other than your communication method.

If prayer isn't about asking for what we want, saying how great we are, or reciting lifeless prayers, then what is it? It's conversation, interaction, engagement, and interchange between two souls who share a mutual respect, love, and admiration for each other. It is free flowing and requires your full presence, just as Spirit offers his full self to the process. If it feels flat or fake you are on the wrong path. Stop and take the time to do some self-assessment, especially in regard to your beliefs about what God thinks of you.

In my spiritual journey I was raised to believe that the preferred posture was facedown in the dirt before Spirit during prayer. I started out feeling separate from and unworthy of the presence of Spirit. Finally I came to understand that Spirit and I were, and always had been, one. Being valuable and worthy of love was my birthright, not something I had to earn. I should be standing face-to-face with Spirit, not prostrate before her. Realizing this revolutionized my practice of prayer. Before it was a chore that I struggled to motivate myself to do. Now it is a constant part of my life, a running dialogue that never stops. I pray in the shower, while I'm driving, in the checkout line at the grocery store, and while I'm waiting for the teakettle to whistle. Most of the time my prayer is silent, but I've been known to mutter under my breath and even speak right out loud. Prayer has shifted from being a way to catch Spirit's attention to a way of elevating myself to a higher level of consciousness and increasing my awareness of connection with her.

If you would like to build an active and vibrant prayer practice that is based on the principles of balance, love, and mutual respect, I suggest you do three things:

1. Talk to Spirit. Share your hopes, dreams, joy, shame, struggles, frustration, exuberance, and humiliation; argue, praise, declare, ask, inform, share, and wax eloquent—whatever it

takes to communicate your authentic self to Spirit is not only appropriate but necessary.

2. Listen to Spirit. Allow her the space and time to speak to you, just as you would anyone else. Listen with your whole being, not just your ears. Spirit uses more than just a still, small voice to communicate with us. She also sends visions, intuitive perceptions, and kinesthetic sensation. If you're earnestly seeking a response that you feel hasn't been sent, ask for a billboard, searchlight, or foghorn. Spirit delights in communicating with us. If we aren't receiving, it's usually because we aren't listening.

3. Be with Spirit. Take time just to exist in the presence of Spirit. Soak up the energy and bask in the warmth. Prayer does not always have to involve an exchange of words. Sometimes when I am in the company of a good friend we are perfectly content to perform separate tasks side by side without conversation. We're happy just to be with someone who loves and accepts us unconditionally. In prayer we can experience the same feeling. Try occasionally to sit and savor Spirit without cluttering the moment with words.

HERE ARE RESOURCES for further instruction on prayer:

How I Pray, edited by Jim Castelli
Castelli interviewed twenty-six spiritual leaders from all faith traditions about their prayer practice. This is an informative, insightful, and often humorous book that will provide you with a wealth of information on different prayer theories, ideas, and practices.

Prayer: Language of the Soul by Phillip Dunn

Dunn combines a discussion of the history, tradition, practice, and theology of prayer with more than 300 selections from all faith traditions. This is one of the most comprehensive books on prayer for the layperson.

Space for God: The Study and Practice of Prayer and Spirituality by Don Postema

Postema has created a beautiful book with illustrations and quotations from a variety of sources. Exercises and suggestions throughout this book involve the mind, body, and soul in the process of prayer. Although written from a Judeo-Christian perspective, it focuses on spirituality rather than doctrine and is therefore easily adapted to all belief systems.

The Centering Prayer

ALTHOUGH THERE are many forms of prayer, I want to address this specific prayer because I think it is very powerful and well suited to our purpose. It focuses on the "being" part of the prayer process. While initially it may seem to be similar to meditation, it's important to remember that just "being" is an important part of the goal of prayer to commune with Spirit. The Centering Prayer's simple focus opens a direct channel to Spirit and allows you to receive an abundance of wisdom. Practicing this form of prayer will provide you with rich inspiration for writing your scripture.

Rooted in the Christian tradition, the concept of the Centering Prayer was first mentioned in *The Cloud of Unknowing*, authored by an anonymous fourteenth-century mystic. He described a process of prayer that involved soul-to-soul contact with Spirit, facilitated by meditation on a word chosen to embody the practitioner's intent on reaching that goal. No other words were necessary; rather they were believed to hinder the process of direct connection with Spirit. In this method of prayer, concentrating on only one word is the key to this connection.

Once relegated to the ranks of priests, nuns, and saints, the Centering Prayer is now being enjoyed by laypersons from all spiritual traditions. If your nature is more contemplative or you want to practice the "being" stage of communicating with Spirit, this is a good method of prayer to select. Because the process is somewhat complex, you may want to read through the instructions at least once before you try it the first time.

1. Find a place and time where you will not be interrupted for about twenty-five minutes.

2. Choose a word, preferably with only one syllable, that represents your intention to unite with Spirit for the highest good imaginable. Some choices might be love, one, faith, or yes. Once you've selected your word, do not change it during the prayer time. If it doesn't work for you, choose another one before your next session. It is preferable that you settle on one word and use it every time you engage in the Centering Prayer.

3. Sit or lie in a position you think you can maintain for the duration of the prayer period, but don't find one so comfortable that you will fall asleep.

4. Close your eyes and take a few deep, even breaths to facilitate relaxation and concentration.

5. Begin gently and silently repeating your word, like a steady rhythm of tiny raindrops falling inside of you. Use the activity to focus on your intention to unite with Spirit in heart and soul rather than in mind.

6. When thoughts intrude, and they will, let them go and return to the process of repeating your word.

7. Continue for twenty minutes.

8. Conclude with a few moments of grounding in the present moment by being increasingly aware of your body, mind, and surroundings.

9. Although this isn't part of the formal Centering Prayer, I encourage you to take the time to jot down some notes about your experience to use in future scripture-writing sessions.

Repeat this process twice a day for twenty minutes. In the beginning, especially if you have no prior experience with contemplative spiritual practices, it will be very difficult to quiet your mind and focus on your intention. That is perfectly normal. Be gentle with yourself. The more you force the process, the harder it will become. Let the intrusions go and peacefully redirect your attention to the repetition of your word.

The Centering Prayer takes practice. You may not have an immediate positive experience with it. But over time, as you become more adept, you will notice an internal shift to a higher level of connection to Spirit.

HERE ARE RESOURCES for further instruction on the Centering Prayer:

Centered: The Handbook of Centering Prayer by Steve Mensing With 114 illustrated pages, this is the obvious choice for all of you visually oriented readers.

*The Centering Prayer: Renewing an Ancient Christian Prayer
Form* by Basil Pennington
This is a classic in the field. Pennington provides a comprehensive discussion of the Centering Prayer that will leave you with a greater appreciation of and confidence in the method.

*Open Mind, Open Heart: The Contemplative Dimension of the
Gospel* by Thomas Keating
Keating believes passionately in the power of the Centering Prayer. He presents an eloquent and practical description of the process that is easy to follow and doesn't expect prior theological knowledge from the reader.

Selecting a Method

PERHAPS YOU'VE BEEN PRACTICING some of these methods and already know which ones best suit the nature of your journey, or maybe in reading about them, one resonated with your Spirit. If you remain confused about where to begin, this chart may be helpful.

Practice	Purpose	Process	Skill Level	Time	Frequency
Guided visualization	Discovery & growth	Imagining	Intermediate	Varies	Varies
Journaling	Expression & growth	Writing	Beginner	Varies	Varies
Lectio Divina	Receiving message from Spirit	Reading, praying, & meditating	Intermediate	Varies	Varies
Transcendental meditation	Attaining *ananda*	Repetition of mantra	Advanced	20 min.	2×/day

Practice	Purpose	Process	Skill Level	Time	Frequency
Vipassana meditation	Attaining nirvana	Focusing on body & mind	Advanced	30 min.	Varies
Prayer	Communion with Spirit	Speaking, listening, & being	Beginner	Varies	Varies
Centering prayer	Unification with Spirit	Repetition of word	Advanced	20 min.	2×/day

I hope you now have at least the beginnings of an idea about which practice to try first as you begin the process of writing your own scripture. Using it will stretch your thinking, creativity, and consciousness in new directions. You may decide to sample each one, but don't tackle more than two at a time. Overwhelming yourself will only serve to sour you on the entire experience. Proceed slowly. Stick with your choices for at least thirty days, unless your immediate reaction is overwhelmingly negative. You may struggle when you first try each method, but don't let that stop you from giving it a chance to work.

THIRTEEN

~

Genres
to Write

JUST AS THERE ARE numerous types of material from
which to take selections of others' work, there are many different genres to choose from when composing your own
scripture. Almost any form of poetry or prose is acceptable, but you may
wish to begin with a genre that you have experience with, such as letter
writing. As you gain confidence, you can start experimenting with
other genres. Allow yourself to start slowly and move at your own pace.
And remember that there is no wrong way to write your own scripture.
Your work need not even directly reference Spirit. The goal is to convey the wisdom and truth you have encountered in your spiritual journey, thus meeting the definition of sacred art and creating a triangular
relationship among you, any readers of your text, and Spirit.

Each of the following genre options will give you some basic instructions and examples. Please note that many of the samples I provide
are far from perfect. That's okay. They don't need to be, and neither
does your work. Personal scripture only needs to adequately capture the

truth you wish to convey. To get an even better sense of the genres, I suggest you read through some of the selections from the chapters listing sacred, spiritual, and secular resources to get a feel for how other authors use them.

Essays

ESSAYS ARE nonfiction pieces written to share and explain an idea or opinion. They are typically short in length, from one to ten pages. Although generally serious in tone, they can be humorous, with even a touch of satire. I like this genre because as a teacher and therapist, it gives me a forum to express many of the ideas that I share with my clients and workshop participants.

To develop an essay, begin with the key thought you want to present. Build your piece around that central theme. For example, when writing about the lessons I had learned from all of my losses, I began a piece with these sentences:

> I have been given such gifts in my life—amazing, awesome, and precious gifts. Gifts that I've opened and rejoiced over and gifts that I haven't even realized I've received yet. They have changed my life. No, they have saved my life, allowing me to not just survive but to thrive despite all of the hurt, betrayal, and loss. I don't believe that Spirit ever gives us such precious gifts to keep to ourselves. So I arrive at this point: recording the gifts I've received so I can share them with others. I want to capture their tremendous power so that maybe I can pass the gift along to someone else who needs it as desperately as I did.

Continue to write about what your subject means to you; explain why you believe in it and why you think others might find it useful to know. Because I am such a visual thinker, I often use metaphors as a basis for my work in this genre. Several essays in my personal sacred text began with a simple proverb or quote and developed as I began to put more thought into why the proverb or quote was important to me. This portion of *Deep Roots of Faith*, an essay I wrote in 1993 and added to my personal sacred text, is an example of one of those:

Several years ago I heard a wonderful quote: "Every great oak was once a nut that stood its ground." While I chuckled at it then, I didn't come to understand the profound truth behind it until later. Within the space of a few short months my world fell apart. I lost my health, my marriage, my financial security, my pride, and my dreams for the future. I also lost some of my faith. During that period there were many, many nights when I prayed as Jesus did in the garden on the Mount of Olives, "Father, if you are willing, take this cup from me" (Luke 22:42).

But He did not. Instead He gave me a greater gift. He got down in the mud-filled pit with me and helped me dig my way out. In the process, we dug deeper pathways for the roots of my faith. Reaching a depth I was not previously aware existed, I found a renewed sense of hope and more ambitious dreams for the future than I ever imagined myself having the courage and capability to achieve!

As a result, I experienced the truth of a seventeenth-century proverb: "A high building, a low foundation." Modern-day architects count on the accuracy of this principle, knowing that a building can only be as tall as it is deep. The same law operates in spirituality. That seed, or nut, that was planted when we acknowledged God as part of our life is limited in its capacity to develop into a mighty oak by the roots that anchor it. Just as it is impossible for a tree to reach great proportions if it is only rooted in an inch of soil, our ability to reach into the world with breadth and height is limited by the depth and width of our faith being anchored in God.

Here's an excerpt from a short essay written by a friend of mine expressing her conflicting emotions and wishes about the relationships in her life. This excerpt is an excellent example of how you can capture wisdom without directly referencing Spirit:

AMBIVALENCE
BY JENNIFER FETTER

He seems so much like me—self-sufficient. But only 'til they meet the perfect one. Run, run, run—give no one the chance to know me. Keep on going—don't stop. You don't really know me. Let me try to explain—but you don't really want to understand me. Tell me what you want and be on your way. What can I do to help? You can't help me—I don't need any help. Leave me alone—hold me close. Don't get too close to me—hold me tight. I want to be alone—leave me alone. Talk to me, let me talk to you. Listen to me—but don't care. No advice please. Give me something to do—don't give me time to think. . . . Delve deeper—into my soul. Search my heart and know me. Love me inside, deeply. Take time out for me. Pay attention to me, not my talents and frivolity. Accept me for me—not what I offer. Love me—simply love me. Unconditionally.

Fiction

FICTION CAN BE a powerful genre to convey a message of wisdom. It can be used to teach a principle, express an opinion, or simply provide an outlet for your feelings. Because it is an indirect method, it usually engages readers with its entertainment value first and then, while they are completely involved in the story, provides an object lesson. The sacred texts of the world are filled with parables and allegories that are used to convey enormous spiritual truth. This genre can be serious or humorous. It can be of any length and take the form of a short story, novel, fable, or parable.

One of my favorite scripture selections in my personal sacred text is a parable I wrote about laughter and the meaning of life. It tells the story of a man who hikes into the mountains one day in a final effort to discern what his existence is all about. In the middle of an isolated meadow he encounters a large box guarded by a solitary soldier. To his amazement the man tells him that the meaning to life is contained in the box. When he opens it, he is greeted by gales of laughter, chuckles, and giggles that knock him to the ground with their strength. While I cannot say that this piece is my finest or contains my greatest wisdom, I do enjoy reading it and sharing it perhaps more than any other because it is simply fun.

Almost a decade ago, while in the midst of my recovery from depression, I wrote an autobiographical fable as part of an assignment for a therapy group. It was about a little girl who lived alone in the desert with no one to comfort her. She believed she had been abandoned there because she was ugly and unlovable. One day a beautiful fairy godmother came and helped her walk a great distance to an oasis. There they crossed under a waterfall and in the process the little girl's tattered clothes and scarred face were restored to perfection. Transformed and renewed, she now lived in a beautiful land with lots of playmates. Years later I am still amazed at what a rich metaphor the story turned out to be for my own spiritual journey.

One of the greatest benefits of fictional scripture writing is that it can be very easy to share because it is both indirect and entertaining. If you want to begin sharing your personal sacred text with someone else in your life and are unsure how that person will respond, choosing a piece of fiction is usually a good place to start. This is also a good genre to use if you are having a hard time finding one to capture a message you want to communicate to others.

Letters

L ETTERS HAVE a lot of the same qualities as essays. The difference is that they are targeted to a specific audience and are friendlier in tone. The epistles in the New Testament of the Bible are good examples of how letters can be used in sacred text.

I often use a correspondence format when I want to respond to an issue that arose from an interaction with someone or someplace in particular. For example, after listening to a sermon that really disturbed me, I was left pondering about my reaction for days afterward. Thinking about it led me to refine my thoughts on the subject of spiritual self-esteem. To capture what I had learned, I sat down and wrote a letter that began like this:

> *A Letter to the Church at Spring Valley:*
> *A little more than a month ago I sat in a chair in your sanctuary. I listened to your pastor tell me I was a wretched and stupid individual, doomed to being so because of my human condition. Although I doubt it was his intent to demean me, his words did just that. You see, I don't believe I'm wretched, or lowly, or doomed. I don't believe my heart was filled with the sin of my forefathers upon my birth. To the contrary, I believe it is my birthright to be filled with joy and confidence in my value.*

I often use letter-writing exercises with my clients. Because these letters are for their personal use, and not intended to be mailed, they are a wonderful outlet for feelings that may not have any other safe means of expression. My client Sarah, having longed for many years to fulfill her dream of becoming a mother, was struggling to find hope and joy in the midst of her waiting. She felt disconnected from feeling Spirit's presence in her darkest moments. She wrote a letter to the baby she hoped to carry one day as a prayer to reconnect:

> *I want to feel your little growing arms and legs moving and bumping against me—inside me. Just to know you are there. I know that every time I am sick or feel nauseous—if I am to feel these symptoms of pregnancy—I will praise God for making you a miracle within me.*

Music and Song

SONGS ARE A frequent part of the world's sacred texts. The Psalms in the Bible's Old Testament and the entire Bhagavad Gita are lyrics intended to be set to music. The opportunity they offer us to express ourselves is doubled when the message is backed by sound.

Unfortunately, neither I nor my clients have tackled this category with much success. The only songs I ever wrote were composed on the swing in my backyard when I was five. There just isn't much call for lyrics about bugs in my personal sacred text. But if this category speaks to you, by all means try it out. You need not have any prior music- or lyric-writing skills. If you have one skill but lack the other, perhaps you will find a partner whose skill complements your own. Or you can write new words to an existing tune. Although I have not experimented much with this genre, I have been able to locate some very good resources for further information:

500 Songwriting Ideas for Brave and Passionate People by Lisa Aschmann
This handy compendium of 500 different ideas can be the starting point for your song-writing exercises.

Songwriting: A Complete Guide to the Craft by Stephen Citron
This is a very well-respected and comprehensive guide to every aspect of the songwriting process—from lyric development to marketing.

Songwriting and the Creative Process: Suggestions and Starting Points for Songwriters by Steve Gillette and Mark Moss
Gillette and Moss have written a basic introduction to the creative process behind songwriting, including many exercises and much concrete advice.

Poetry

THE PURPOSE OF poetry is not usually to explain an opinion or teach a specific point. It is more typically used as a means of creatively expressing oneself, regardless of whether there is an audience or not. It can be fiction or nonfiction, serious or humorous, and only a few lines in length or of epic proportion.

Poetry is the genre that I have the most difficulty getting my clients to explore. A lot of people have had negative experiences reading or writing poetry in their past. At times, it can be a difficult category to understand, more so than straightforward essays or stories, because it relies heavily on imagery and sound rather than linear logic.

The great paradox is that poetry can be one of the most freeing writing experiences you will have because it truly has so few rules. You can use sentence fragments, any structure you like, and punctuation is not required. Because poetry relies so heavily on sensory input to convey its message, it does not have to follow many of the grammatical and structural rules that dominate other genres. Consequently, I try to get everyone to start writing his or her own scripture in a poetry format.

I could teach you the meaning of mysterious terms such as assonance, consonance, and iambic pentameter, but those would only further any misconceptions that poetry is a difficult genre to understand and write. Knowing what these terms mean is not a necessary prerequisite to capturing your truth in poetic style.

Instead, I want you to focus on only two simple concepts: imagery and sound. Poetry reading and writing should be a mystical process. Build something that creates a sensual experience by incorporating elements that appeal not just to the rational mind but to the senses as well. Use metaphors and word pictures in your poetry that draw your reader into your message. Don't choose something so obscure that no one will be able to relate. Instead, select a versatile image that you use repeatedly. For example, when I was a child I was often told that I was too sensitive. I grew up thinking it was a character flaw. As an adult I finally realized it was an asset, but one I had to balance with wisdom. In this excerpt you can see that I used the image of a heart to convey my message:

A HEART CLOAKED IN WISDOM

I disowned my heart
   Cut it out of my chest with a knife
   Made sharp by the shame and condemnation of others and
   Buried it under layers of soil in my childhood yard
And then the depression came
   For without my heart I could feel
   Neither the pain nor the joy
   I had amputated my capacity to breathe the freshness of the air
   To feel the warmth of the sun upon my face
I went back and dug up my heart
   Only to give it away to the first man who would have me

The use of sound is another sensory experience you can incorporate into your poetry. When the words are spoken aloud, they can have a rhythm consistent with their content. For example, if the poem is strong and direct, it might have short staccato phrases. If it is eloquent it might have a relaxed, almost lyrical pacing. Choosing a rhyming pattern can give your poem a humorous or playful tone.

My friend Margaret wrote this poem. You can almost feel the comforting message it conveys:

HOW I SEE
BY MARGARET MALONEY

I look at others and myself
Through a grid of shame.
I see how I'm no good and
Don't measure up.

I believe I am what I do,
So I become a master performer.
I believe what you do,
Says something about me.
How I could make you different,
If I tried harder . . .

Now I see through a
Veil of Grace.
I am not what I do.
I am not responsible for
How others respond or behave.
I am good not because of me
But because God created me
In His image.
I am a child of God.
Part of His family.
A treasure in His eyes!

By contrast, Jennifer, who wrote the previous essay on ambivalence, continued to capture what she was learning about relationships in this untitled poem whose first section actually sounds confusing and chaotic by the way its meter and structure changes:

Sometimes I feel You fading fast
Into the clouds of my faithlessness
Sometimes I lose You in the crowd
When I open myself up to another's caress.
Sometimes I feel so all alone
And fall into the well of dejection.

If you decide that you want to write poetry but are unsure of how to proceed, go back to the chapters listing spiritual and secular resources and find some poetry works that appeal to you. One of the best ways to

learn how to write poetry is to read it. If that fails to give you the help
you need, check out these resources for further instruction:

Finding What You Didn't Lose: Expressing Your Truth and
Creativity through Poem-Making by John Fox
This is my favorite book on writing poetry and the only one
I recommend to my clients and workshop participants.
Fox does a superb job of teaching his readers how to create
heartfelt and eloquent poetry without getting mired in tech-
nique.

The Teachers and Writers Handbook of Poetic Forms, edited by
Ron Padgett
This resource lists every form of poetry known to humans. It
describes how to write each form and provides examples of
each.

Prayer

PRAYER IS BOTH a simple and a vast category. Prayers can be just
a few sentences of heartfelt expression, or they can be songs with
ten stanzas. Although their format can vary widely, their purpose is always the same: to communicate with Spirit. When you write scripture
in this genre you can choose any style or approach you like; the only
guideline is that it should complement the content of your message. For
example, you would not want to use an epic poem to ask for assistance
building a simpler life or use a satirical essay to seek a miracle of healing
for your child.

My friend Margaret wrote this prayer modeled after Psalm 139
when she was facing issues about weight loss and body image:

O Lord, you have searched me and you know me. You know when
I eat and when I drink, you know my desire and obsession with

food. You know my desire to know you. You are familiar with my ways. You have laid your hand upon me. You anoint me with your Spirit and you tell me when I am hungry and when I am full. Such knowledge is too wonderful for me. Where can I go from your Spirit? Where can I flee from your presence? Wherever I go and whatever I eat you know. I can't hide my binge from you even in my dark closet. Even there your light shines. Even darkness is light to you. You created all my hunger pains and know exactly what my body needs, for you created my innermost being. How precious to me are your thoughts and the growls you send me to let me know I am hungry.

Proverbs

PROVERBS ARE the easiest and simplest of the genres to write. They are very brief quotations or statements that capture truth. Proverbs are often humorous, using puns or wordplays to make their point. They are one of my favorite categories, probably because the wisdom in these brief statements is so accessible. I've memorized several proverbs and repeat them to myself as affirmations or encouragement, such as "Your feelings are not your fault" and "My intuition is my friend." My clients get very tired of hearing the proverbs I have constructed and often roll their eyes at me whenever I repeat them yet again.

One of my most treasured selections in my personal sacred text is a picture I drew of a strand of pearls. It is titled "The Gifts of Grief." Within each bead is written a proverb, in a circular pattern, that represents something I have learned as a result of processing the losses I have faced. For example, one says, "Listen to me to follow me, not to lead me." Another reads, "I want is not the same as I need."

· · ·

NOW YOU ARE EQUIPPED with all of the tools you need to write your own scripture. If you are still a bit unsure, start with something simple like a letter or a proverb. As you begin to feel more confident, explore other genres. Soon you will be a prolific and accomplished scripture writer.

~

PART FIVE

Using Your Personal Sacred Text

You will know the truth,
and the truth shall set you free.

— THE BIBLE,

JOHN 8:32

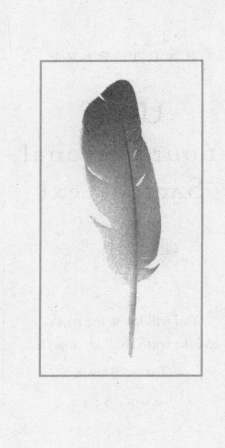

FOURTEEN

Individual
Processes

YOU HAVE BEEN learning a great deal as you explore,
read, and write about your spiritual life. Discoveries and
new lessons learned result in an incredible excitement, one
you need to capitalize on and use to enrich your journey. One of the
greatest lessons I have learned in my life is that finding wisdom is only
half the experience. Taking that wisdom and integrating it into my life
is the second, and often overlooked, part of the process of creating my
personal sacred text. If you go to the effort of exploring new beliefs and
challenging old ones, it will all be moot if you do not take what you encounter and allow it to change you. In order to do that, you have to use
your text in a way that promotes your interaction with the material on
intellectual, emotional, and spiritual levels.

It's important that you start this process with your first selection.
Don't wait until you have completed your text. Integrating the material
into your life is a key power source for the self-perpetuating forward motion involved in creating a personal sacred text. The new wisdom you

obtain will alter and motivate your journey. Waiting until the end of your travels to use your text will result in a less satisfying and shallower experience. Don't cheat yourself out of the benefits creating your personal sacred text has for you.

There are numerous ways to integrate the material in your personal sacred text into your life experience. Those I detail in this chapter—memorization, reflection, realigning your compass, and envisioning the future—have proven to be the most successful for my clients and me. Memorization and reflection are suited to using individual selections in your text, while realigning your compass and envisioning the future are suited toward your text as a whole.

Memorization

AS A CHILD, I spent many hours memorizing Bible verses, prayers, and various parts of the Catholic catechism. At the time it seemed fruitless, if not actually tortuous. I saw no value in the repetitious recitation of those things, except to earn the approval of the nuns and priests. Every Sunday I listened to the congregation repeat its contribution to the Mass, and even at my young age I heard the hollow sincerity in their intonation. It seemed that the more times we recited something from memory, the more meaning it lost.

I remember attending my grandmother's funeral services where the priest led us through the rosary in record speed. Before any of us knew what hit us, he had finished and dashed out the building leaving us with our mouths hanging open. The older women from Grandma's generation were asking one another, "I think he miscounted. Did you follow him, dear?"

Unfortunately, I allowed these early experiences to color my perception of the tool of memorization. I generalized that all memorization must be wrong and rejected its continued usefulness. I reacted as I had reacted to other bad experiences in my life: I swung to the opposite extreme of the position and refused to memorize anything having to do with my faith. I wanted every part of my prayer and worship to be spontaneous and without rigid regulation.

Several years ago I stumbled on a group of people who were exploring the use of poetry as a means to express their spirituality. As I listened to them read their poems, this creative tool immediately captivated me. Here, it seemed, was something that could offer me a new creative freedom to commune with and about Spirit. But then irony struck as I heard them talk of the power of committing their poems to memory as a part of the spiritual practice. I kept listening and had to agree that what they said made sense. Once again Spirit found a way to guide me from an unhealthy place at an extreme edge into a wiser middle ground.

Now I not only use memorization in my spiritual practice but wholeheartedly encourage others to do so as well. There is a reason that anchoring something in your long-term recall is euphemistically referred to as learning it "by heart" or "committing" it to memory. The process you undertake requires that you actually integrate the words into your experience. The human brain stores information by a process of categorization. Every piece of data that comes into your cognition is analyzed, sorted, and matched up with an already established file of related information. If the material seems totally unique, a new "folder" is established, but even it has to be linked to one already in existence in order for the brain's web of connections to work properly. With each new addition you actually alter the neural pathways that control your thought processes.

When you memorize something you set this process in motion. The words get associated with and incorporated into a previously gathered collection of material. As a result, you are changed by what you learn and it becomes a part of you. Do you remember from chapter 3 the Hindu path of union with Spirit referred to as bhakti yoga (page 34)? It is the process of coming to know Spirit through discernment and intuition that leads, over time, to becoming more closely conformed to Spirit. Memorization embraces the same concept because it allows us to incorporate new material into our being. As a result, we are changed.

Since integrating what you put into your personal sacred text is one of the primary goals for creating it, learning some of it word for word becomes an invaluable tool in seeing this become a reality.

Aside from the transformational qualities, memorization has the added benefit of making your personal sacred text portable and easily accessible under any circumstances. During difficult, puzzling, or joyful situations you can readily locate a source of wisdom without having to find, or even have in your possession, your book. If the kids are screaming, the kitchen sink is backing up, and you have company coming in ten minutes, you can recite a particular poem or passage that brings you peace. When you see an incredible sunset and are awed by the majesty of the world Spirit created, you will be able to say that wonderful prayer of thanksgiving you found several years ago. Your sacred text will be as close as your own memory!

Be wary of falling into mindless recitation, like the masses of my childhood. Take care to keep your heart, as well as your mind, engaged in the process. If you find yourself repeating words but not experiencing any associated feelings, then you are treading on the grounds of insincerity. Drop that selection from your repertoire for a while and either choose another less tired piece or move into spontaneous communion with Spirit.

Reflection

YOU WILL UNDOUBTEDLY be putting a great deal of careful thought into the selection and writing of your personal sacred text. That is certainly one aspect of reflection. But for the purposes of this chapter, the term refers to introspection about the pieces after you've selected them.

As part of my history as a Catholic school student and seminarian, I engaged in a great deal of Bible study. Through class assignments, small-group involvement, and personal investigation I became closely acquainted with the messages contained in this particular sacred text. Reading, researching, and analyzing different passages greatly contributed to my understanding of it. At times this review included not only the active process of searching the text for meaning but also silently reflecting and seeking further wisdom related to the message through prayer and meditation. If you have belonged to an organized religion for any length of time, you probably have experienced a similar type of study.

The process of using reflection to integrate the material from your personal sacred text into your life involves a similar active and receptive process. Each piece deserves a closer look that involves searching for new layers of meaning and application. You may have done some of these actions when you first wrote or selected the piece, but now that it is a part of your sacred text, you are ready for a much closer look. Try these few steps to explore your work in depth:

1. Read and reread the selected piece. Try doing it silently and then aloud. Become intimately familiar with the words. Underline and highlight passages that catch your attention. Scribble notes in the margins about thoughts that come into your head.

2. Ask questions. If the selection was written by someone else, take the time to do some research into its history and the author's background. When and why was it written? What were the circumstances surrounding its development? What was the author's motivation in writing the piece? What was the meaning or significance of the piece to the author and the immediate audience? What is your interpretation of the meaning based on your interaction with it? Read other works by the same author if you have time. Doing so will help you get a more complete picture of him or her. Keep track of what you find in the margins, on a blank facing page, or in your journal.

3. If you wrote the selection, "detach" yourself from it and try approaching it from the standpoint of a cultural anthropologist. Ask yourself the same sorts of questions that you did in step 2. Be sure to record your thoughts too. Those written records will become invaluable in tracing your immediate thought process and overall spiritual development.

4. Once you feel that you have a good grasp on the piece and its meaning, use this phase of the reflective process to seek Spirit wisdom and guidance. One of the methods you learned or were previously familiar with from chapter 12 would be a good way to achieve those ends. Prayer, meditation, and Lectio Divina are all excellent tools for seeking Spirit guidance and wisdom from passages in your personal sacred text.

5. Prior to or during this time ask Spirit to reveal to you any additional meaning that would be beneficial. I always request clarity of vision and heightened sensory perception so that I can better interpret what might be right in front of me. I have a friend who asks Spirit for billboards and spotlights if she is struggling to find meaning from a particular message.

6. Seek wisdom and guidance for what to do with the meaning once it becomes clear. Is there a particular action that you should take as a result of your new understanding? If so, how and when is it best for you to do that? Perhaps it's just a matter of storing the information for later. Ask Spirit to help you recall it when the time is right. Continue to journal or note the directions you receive.

Reflection for the purpose of seeking meaning and wisdom is often a cyclical process. You may think you have exhausted the benefits of a piece entirely only to find at a later point that it speaks to something entirely different. As this is often the case, you will want to review every selection periodically so that you don't miss an opportunity to enjoy it from a fresh angle. If you continue to approach your text with an open and receptive mind, Spirit will never exhaust the ways you will be able to reflect on it.

Realigning Your Compass

ALL OF US reach points in our lives, some of us more frequently than others, where we feel that we might be headed in the wrong direction. This might be precipitated by a specific idea about what is amiss and why, or it might take shape as a vague, intuitive knowing that is more amorphous than a clear vision. Your personal sacred text can help you find your way in either situation.

This is an opportunity to put all of your notes, documentation, and journal writing to good use. If, for example, you have a relationship that seems headed in the wrong direction, look for developments in your selections or own writing that are related to that topic. Search through your work for patterns and themes. Did you start out the relationship with a spurt of pieces about trust and partnership but now see a movement into ones that speak of loneliness or isolation?

As I review my own sacred text I continue to be amazed at how my own process is clearly reflected. Even though my volume is sorted by genre rather than chronologically, I can still chart my course of moving from difficult times to better times and then sliding back again. When I was taking care of my own needs rather than bowing to the demands of others, there was confidence and hope in my work. When I slipped back into codependent behavior, my views became pessimistic.

Seeing myself waffling on a particular issue in black and white is hard to ignore and gives me significant motivation to stay on track. It also provides me with the information I need to figure out why I might be getting off the road in the first place. Gradually I learn what was going on for me and I am able to avoid it in the future. My clients and I often review their texts for the same types of developments when they are feeling stuck or at an impasse in therapy.

Visioning the Future

JUST AS IT is not unusual to encounter moments of feeling that you might be headed down the wrong path, there will be times when you don't know what the future holds for you. That point might come before you choose a particular route or after you've realized you've been on the wrong road and now need to back up and choose again. For example, you could be deciding between married and single life, or what to do with your marriage now that you've realized it isn't reaching its full potential.

I am a firm believer in establishing dreams and goals for the future. They should not be so rigid as to lock you into something for time eternal, but their absence will leave you unfocused in a world that moves you along so swiftly that before you know it, half your life is gone and you don't feel like you've accomplished anything of substance. Clearly defined goals have a mighty capacity to influence the universe. It is with our intention and commitment that we can consciously act in our lives rather than passively accept or reactively respond to whatever comes our way. *Building Your Field of Dreams* by the Reverend Mary Manin Morrissey eloquently discusses the power and purpose of this topic.

Once you have determined that you need and want some help setting your vision for the future, analyze your text. Look for patterns as I discussed in the last section. This time, though, focus specifically on those subjects or ideas that seem to give you the greatest peace, joy, and feelings of vibrant energy. If you want to know what career interests to pursue, seek vocational themes, such as helping other people or group leadership. Where is it in your writing that you see yourself come alive with enthusiasm? Search those items for clues.

When you get an initial hint, stop at that passage and use the reflection process of study and seeking wisdom. You may have to go through this search and reflection process more than once. Over time a picture will emerge from which you can gain the insight you need to step forward into your future confident that you are on the right path. Continue to ask and look as you go, though, in case the road has a turn or an exit you shouldn't miss!

Choosing a Method

LIKE MANY of the other options presented in this book, those presented in this chapter can be altered, combined, or adjusted to suit your needs. Feel free to experiment with them. You might find a new one that is perfect for you, or you might create an amalgamation of two or three. There are no rules, only best possible matches for a particular person at a specific point in time. As long as you are achieving the goal of integrating your personal text into your life, then you can consider your method successful.

When my client Susan encounters a difficult situation, she uses a combination of the methods of memorization and realigning your compass. She memorizes an appropriate proverb from her sacred text and uses it to refocus her life. For example, she selected Marcel Proust's "The real voyage of discovery consists not in seeking new landscapes but in having new eyes" and then spent an afternoon looking through the recent scripture pieces she had written, easily identifying alternative ways of viewing her current challenges. When she encountered difficult circumstances throughout the course of the day, she could repeat the proverb to herself and be instantly reminded of her ability to rise above the problem and see it with a fresh perspective.

I often use the process of realigning my compass in conjunction with envisioning the future. When I review my text and see a lot of my recent pieces reflecting anger, such as they did after my divorce, I know I need both to let go of that emotion and to embrace one that will give me more positive energy. After the divorce, I had been carrying anger around for so long that to simply release it without replacing it would have left me feeling very tempted to pick it back up. You will soon recognize these same types of behavior and thought patterns within yourself and will quickly develop the ability to combine the methods of using your text that best enhance and enrich your life.

ALL OF THE TOOLS mentioned in this chapter are solitary pursuits. Perhaps you have chosen to share your journey with someone else, maybe even a group of people. Before we end this adventure, let's take a look at the ways you can maximize your communal experience with your personal sacred text.

FIFTEEN

Community
Involvement

DECIDING WITH WHOM and how to share your personal sacred text is one of the most important decisions you will make in the whole creation process. This point has more guidelines and cautions attached to it than any other activity in this book because it crosses the line from a private action to a public one. The thoughts and feelings you are choosing to share with someone else are intensely personal. Their revelation will leave you vulnerable to judgment about concepts that are part of your core value system. For this reason, caution is warranted.

However, when done in the appropriate way with the right people, sharing your personal sacred text with others can be immensely rewarding. Others can give you valuable feedback on what you've written. Sharing material with someone will open a dialogue that results in your learning new perspectives and discovering avenues to explore that you had previously not considered. The lives of those you share with will be enriched by what you have learned. And, perhaps most important, sharing your selections with others is a very personal revelation that will create a stronger bond between you and those you care about.

Should I Share My Text?

I HAD BEEN QUIETLY gathering material into my personal sacred text for years before I considered sharing it with someone else. My reluctance to reveal my discoveries was due to the bad experiences I had in the past when I bucked the trends of my faith tradition. Since so much of what I had assembled was contrary to the teachings of the denomination I was practicing in at that time, I doubted that any public sharing would be met with warmth and encouragement. Determining if I should venture out and share my text was a very calculated decision for me.

For you, the same amount of careful consideration may not be necessary. Perhaps you have healthy relationships in place that allow you to openly express yourself. You may belong to a spiritual tradition that welcomes explorations and personal discoveries no matter what path they take. Or you may be finding confirmation that what you currently believe and practice is right for you. If this is the case, it is likely you will not have much risk of being judged if you share your text within your current faith community.

However easy the decision to share your text with others may appear, I urge you to read through the rest of this chapter before you proceed. I have had clients leave my office with great confidence that someone in their life would be a safe and accepting audience for their work only to see them return the next week intensely disappointed by the experience. You have worked too hard up to this point to risk having your journey derailed by rejection and judgment. Do, therefore, proceed with care.

Remember, *not* sharing your text with someone at any point in the journey is an acceptable choice. Your sacred text is an extremely personal process, and whether it remains private or becomes public is your decision. Will your experience be less rich than the experience of others who choose to share their text? Perhaps. There is no guarantee that it will or won't. What I *can* promise is this: If you do not have a safe and accepting person or community to share with, keeping it to yourself is better than having a negative experience.

What is your motive? The single best way to determine whether you are ready to share your text with someone else is to examine your motive in doing so. Do not proceed if your intentions are anything other than to share the joy of your discoveries and receive validating support.

Are you trying to impress someone? If you're seeking to impress someone, you're better off taking up bodybuilding. Are you only trying to show off your writing skills? Then choose something from your collection other than a piece you've written for your sacred text. Do you want to show the world how literate you are? Satisfy that need by waxing eloquent in any number of other verbal or written forums. Mixing ego into the process of sharing your sacred text only reflects that you misunderstood the purpose of creating it from the beginning.

Are you trying to convert someone? Your personal sacred text is not about converting someone to your way of thinking either. The whole process is so rooted in respect for individual choice that to use it in this manner is hypocritical. Save sharing your sacred text for inviting others to have a glimpse of your spiritual world rather than for forcing them to ascribe to what you believe.

Are you seeking approval or guidance by sharing? Proceed with caution if your motive is to seek approval, guidance, or feedback on your path from others. This is a personal and individual journey that only you, in partnership with Spirit, should direct. Unless the person you are seeking input from knows you well and possesses a strong sense of intuitive wisdom, I doubt he or she can point you in any direction that you wouldn't be better off finding for yourself. Those decisions are part of the learning and growth process.

Although you may not purposely approach the process of seeking feedback with the intention of surrendering control over the direction of your text, it is prudent to avoid putting yourself in positions where the influence would be powerful but indirect or subconscious. I worked with a young woman who chose to share a poem from her text with her dad. Although her overt intention was not to seek his approval or guidance, he was such a strong authority figure in her life that his response colored the decisions she made from that point forward about what and how to explore.

Whom Should I Share My Personal Sacred Text With?

As you will likely choose more than one person or group throughout your lifetime, making that choice is a process that you may cycle through several times. The first time will be the most challenging.

To begin, I recommend that you choose one person, rather than a group, with whom you have a degree of trust and familiarity. It isn't necessary that he or she know your heart and soul or be your best friend. In fact, sometimes it's easier to start with someone you have a little distance from rather than your partner or closest confidante, especially if what you have to share is a vast departure from how you typically express yourself. And remember to give yourself a chance to practice your delivery, if you need to.

Whenever I characterize the person I think my clients should select to initially share pieces of their text with it ends up sounding like the perfect description of a Boy Scout or an Irish setter. You should seek someone who is trustworthy, accepting, and respectful of others. Avoid people who aren't good listeners, have little tolerance for thoughts or ideas different from their own, and wouldn't be able to keep what you share in confidence if that is important to you.

Some good choices to consider may be a friend, family member, therapist, spiritual leader, or clergy person. My first selection was my therapist because I could count on her to receive this gift without judgment. I also knew that she would help me sort through my thoughts about the piece and where I would go from there without imposing her own ideas on the process. By sharing your text you are giving someone a precious gift. Choose a person who will receive it graciously.

Informal Methods for Sharing Your Text

THERE ARE TWO basic ways of presenting your material to your audience: in person or via an indirect method of communication, such as e-mail. I suggest the former because it allows you to interact with your listener in a way that gives you a wealth of feedback, not just from the person's words but from body language and voice intonation as well. Consider reading your work aloud so that the person has the opportunity to hear the message in your voice, with the inflection and emphasis that you intended it to have. I also recommend that your first-time sharing involve only a piece or two from your book rather than the entire thing. Control what you will read and in what order, at least until you witness the person's initial reactions.

After you have developed a trust in the exchange, you can consider providing selections by indirect methods such as fax, letter, e-mail, or even audiotape. You may choose to start with one of these indirect methods, either because it's more convenient or provides a feeling of safety. Perhaps there already is a great enough trust between you and the person you choose to share your work with that you will not find it necessary to be present. Or perhaps circumstances preclude your being there in person and you would rather present the piece indirectly than wait for the direct opportunity.

If you are unsure of how the person will respond and do not want to be there when your work is read, I recommend you take a second look at your decision to reveal yourself to this person. However, if you are certain sharing part of your personal sacred text with this individual is the right thing, then sharing it indirectly is a better choice than not doing it at all. This is your process and I wholeheartedly believe you will know what is best in every situation.

Formal Methods for Sharing Your Text

SHARING YOUR WORK with others individually on an informal basis may provide you with periodic support, but if you are seeking ongoing encouragement, I suggest you consider establishing a formal relationship with at least one other person engaged in creating his or her own sacred text. Since you will be united in your creative process, you will be able to provide one another with support in ways that those not assembling their texts will not. You can exchange resources you've discovered, spiritual practices that were particularly successful, and creative solutions to problems encountered along the way. Plus, you will be able to benefit from the extra energy generated when two or more people are gathered in a united purpose.

PARTNERSHIPS

IS THERE SOMEONE in your life who shares your desire to create a personal sacred text? Does that person also have the ability to build with you a safe and supportive relationship that empowers both of you toward spiritual and personal growth? Are your schedules similar enough that you can meet together for an hour or two at least every other week? If so, then you may have an ideal situation for forming a partnership.

If safety and intimacy are primary concerns, I suggest you start building your support for this process by establishing a partnership. Choose someone with whom you already have a mutually supportive relationship and a shared desire for spiritual growth. If your partner isn't already familiar with the process of creating a personal sacred text, describe it to him or her and ask if he or she would be interested in undertaking the project too. While you will not be moving along identical paths, you can provide each other with invaluable encouragement and wisdom, making your separate paths much easier to travel.

During your initial session, discuss basic elements, such as when you will meet, how often, and where. I recommend you come together every week or every other week. If the gap is any wider, you risk spending too much of your time catching up rather than constructively moving forward. If you meet once a week, an hour to ninety minutes should be plenty of time. Should you choose to meet every other week, I suggest you block out two hours.

The goal of your first few gatherings will be to establish a mutual understanding of how your partnership will function and how you can best empower each other. You should each take the time to explain your hopes and goals for the process, along with expectations and ideas about how the partnership can support them. Exchange your spiritual histories briefly if you aren't already acquainted with that part of each other's background.

While the agenda of subsequent meetings can take a variety of forms, I have found it best to provide each person with time to share both their process developments and their selections. These two topics can be combined into one sharing time or two separate rounds of sharing. Talk to each other about what you have been exploring, difficulties you encounter, wisdom you gain, and lessons you learn. Feedback should be supportive and nonjudgmental. Giving advice is not allowed unless both partners consent to it being a part of the process. The depth and detail of what is shared is up to each person. Allow you and your partner the time to settle into a routine that benefits both of your sacred text goals.

GROUPS

WHILE AT TIMES complicated to organize and maintain, a group can add a great deal of energy and strength to creating your sacred text. At some time in your life you probably have seen a flock of geese traveling across the sky in a V-shaped pattern. Rotating turns at taking the head of the V, sharing their flight, makes it possible for the flock to travel 71 percent farther and faster than a single goose could on its own.

Belonging to a group assembled for the purpose of supporting one another in the process of creating personal sacred texts can have the same benefit. You will learn from one another's successes and failures, and the wheel won't always have to be reinvented. The encouragement and collective wisdom you receive from every single member will empower you to move more quickly and productively than if you traveled fueled only by your own energy.

The problem is that it's harder to find several like-minded people to form a group than it is just one for a partnership. You will need to locate others who not only share your vision for spiritual growth but who also have the maturity needed to facilitate a healthy group's functioning *and* a schedule compatible with your own. Most of my clients have wanted to be part of a group during the process of creating their sacred text, but very few have been lucky enough to do so. It took me years to find a group that suited my desires and needs.

If you feel a group is right for you, don't let the difficulty of finding or establishing one deter you from the task. It may fall together just perfectly right away, or it may take several efforts over a longer period of time. As you persist in your endeavors, find alternative sources of support, such as a partnership, or find others who aren't creating a sacred text but who will encourage you as you do so.

Given that the concept of creating a personal sacred text is new, it is not too likely that you will find a group already in existence in your area. Check my website, www.riveroftruth.com, for listings of established groups that are willing to accept new members. Probably you will have to create a group.

There are three basic elements to keep in mind throughout the process of creating a group: membership, meetings, and ground rules. Each is an important consideration in any group's development. As a therapist and workshop leader, I tend to all three areas each time I form a group.

Group Size: Before beginning to look for members, decide how large you want your group to be. A smaller group may be more intimate, but it will likely have less energy. I recommend you aim for four to eight people. If you have fewer people, you risk needing to cancel the meetings when someone can't make it. When a group is any larger, it's difficult to form a cohesive bond and people don't get adequate time to share. If you must have larger numbers, consider breaking into smaller groups for sections of each meeting.

There are a variety of factors to keep in mind when considering whom to invite to join your group. First and foremost, these individuals will need to be in on the process of creating their personal sacred text or be willing to begin doing so. Again, because the concept is new, you might have to explain the process often as you seek interested participants.

Compatible Backgrounds for Members: While it isn't necessary that each person you choose share your exact spiritual beliefs and values, it is important that their beliefs and values are compatible with your own. An individual who practices in a Pagan tradition may not feel accepted and supported in a group of Evangelical Christians. Orthodox Jews may not always be comfortable with Buddhists. This doesn't imply that one tradition is better, worse, or even intolerant, just that they have some fundamental differences that may not be completely conducive to forming a cohesive group. Variety may be a wonderful stimulant for growth, but it is also important that each member feels comfortable enough to freely express him- or herself without judgment or conflict. Try to strike a balance between similarity and difference when assembling your membership roster. I have had several wonderful experiences with groups that consisted of very eclectic memberships including Buddhists, Protestants, and Pagans. Their open-minded and accepting attitudes made all the difference between a dysfunctional and rewarding experience for all involved.

Consider personal characteristics such as gender, marital status, and sexual orientation when developing your group. Would you feel more comfortable in a group composed of individuals like you in these respects? Perhaps the opposite is true, and you would find yourself motivated by the stories and wisdom of people from a variety of lifestyles and backgrounds. Like most of the choices presented in this book, the right one is not predetermined but depends on your personal preferences.

Commitment: Choose members who are willing and are able to make a commitment to the group. Members who come and go without regularity will greatly impact the dynamics of the group, and most of the consequences are negative. A consistent membership is needed to build the trust, intimacy, and rapport necessary to support the group process. It is impossible to entirely eliminate the possibility that someone will drop out unexpectedly. You can, however, minimize the risk of accepting an uncommitted member by explaining your expectations about attendance up front and seeking information about each individual's schedule and prior history as a group member.

Scheduling: In these busy and hectic days it is difficult to find times when several people are free to meet. For this reason, it is important that schedule considerations be part of your membership selection process rather than something that follows. While it may be sad to eliminate someone from consideration who meets all of your other expectations but has no time free on the one day everyone else does, it is important to remember that no one benefits if an accessible meeting time cannot be established.

Qualified Members: It is important to select group members who have the skills and desire to be a constructive part of the process. These two qualities are equally important. Someone may have the emotional and spiritual maturity needed to contribute, but if he or she doesn't want to participate, that person's presence is more of a hindrance than an asset. On the other hand, a member with the desire to contribute but who monopolizes the group's time or consistently demonstrates passive-aggressive behavior can derail the entire process. Ideally, you will choose potential members from people you know from prior group experiences or whom you are familiar enough with individually to gauge their skill and desire level.

Closed versus Open Membership: Once you have found members for your group, you will need to consider whether your group will be closed or open. A closed group will not accept new members. An open group will accept new members if they meet your requirements. A closed group will usually allow you to build greater intimacy and trust because the membership is consistent. However, each addition to an open group brings new wisdom and energy. The choice depends on the wishes of your membership. You can start out as one or the other and change in the future if the majority agrees.

Meetings: Choose a consistent time, day, and place for your meetings, such as every Tuesdays from seven to nine at Susie's. This will give everyone a chance to build it into his or her schedule. Ask members to bring their calendars to each meeting in case changes need to be made. I suggest that you gather every week or bimonthly, such as every second and fourth Tuesday. The amount of time you'll need will vary depending on the number of group members. Small groups may be able to accomplish everything in ninety minutes, but larger groups will need at least two hours.

During your initial gatherings spend some time getting to know one another and establishing the structure of the group and the meeting. Give people a chance to introduce themselves and give any background information they feel is relevant. Ask them to talk about why they are there, what they hope to gain from the process, and how they think the group can best support them. Use a white board or large tablet of paper to write things down if you have a lot of visually oriented group members.

During this first meeting decide whether you will have a leader, and, if so, who that will be and how the role will be defined. If you don't want anything that formal, a good option is to have a facilitator position that rotates from week to week. This individual would be responsible for keeping the meeting on time and moving along. Duties such as making sure the ground rules are followed should remain with the whole membership. Most groups I run and help establish use this type of leadership model.

The initial gathering is also the place to decide the format of your meetings. If you choose to form a story circle, sacred circle, Master Mind group, or Road Warrior group described later in the chapter, that may be decided for you. But if not, you'll need to design at least a loose plan for how you will spend your time. I generally recommend that gatherings begin with a brief check-in period, allowing all members to say how they're feeling and what may have transpired in their lives since the last meeting. This doesn't have to be specifically related to their activities of creating a personal sacred text but can be a time to update one another on life's larger joys, difficulties, and issues. Be careful to stress the brevity of this activity. I have watched more than one group get bogged down in the check-ins and never get into the body of the meeting.

The remaining time can be spent in much the same way that I recommended partnership meetings be conducted. Everyone should have the opportunity to share his or her progress and to read any selections made or written. Again, this can be done in a single round of sharing or in two rounds. Advice and/or feedback should be offered only if the individual asks for it or if the group decides these activities will be a part of the process. Participation is always optional, and a member can pass up a turn at any time.

Plan a short closing activity to end the meeting on an upbeat and affirming note. At times the sharing in your group will be intense, emotional, and theoretical. An ending ritual will give the group a chance to refocus and get grounded. A prayer, song, or poem that can be recited or sung together is a good option. I have also seen members close by exchanging affirmations or prayer requests.

Ground Rules: Ground rules provide a unified and public acknowledgment of expectations for members' behavior. They create a sense of safety and, consequently, allow trust to build.

Based on my years of professional experience leading groups, I have put together a list of standard ground rules that I use repeatedly. I explain them to everyone during our first meeting so boundaries are clearly established from the outset. The group is always invited to use a consensus process to modify the rules I provide or add any additional ground rules they feel appropriate.

Use these rules as a starting point for developing the ground rules for your own group. They are by no means a comprehensive or required list. Although they have been time-tested, they may not be perfectly suited to your particular group. I recommend that you discuss the rules during your first meeting even if you don't settle on a final format until a week or two after everyone has had a chance to think about them and add input. I suggest reading the agreed-upon list of rules aloud at the beginning of every meeting.

1. Group members will be on time for meetings and let the group's facilitator know in advance if they will not be present.

2. Group members will use respectful language at all times. Put-downs, verbal attacks, and interruptions are examples of unacceptable communication.

3. Group members will behave toward one another in a respectful manner at all times. Unwanted physical contact and monopolizing the conversation are examples of unacceptable behavior.

4. Group members will offer support, acceptance, and encouragement rather than judgment or unsolicited advice.

5. Group members will keep confidential whatever is shared during the meetings.

6. Group members will discuss conflicts or difficulties directly with the person involved rather than other parties, and work constructively to resolve those differences.

7. Group members will commit themselves to their own growth and to empowering the growth of other members. This includes doing whatever individual work is necessary to facilitate that process.

8. If at any time a member wishes to no longer be committed to the group's purpose, he or she will excuse him- or herself from membership.

GROUP MODELS

THERE ARE FOUR group models you can use if you are not inclined to create your own: story circles, sacred circles, Master Mind groups, and Road Warrior groups. Although not all are specifically designed for sharing the process of creating your personal sacred text, their focus on supporting personal and spiritual growth in a group format makes them easily adaptable. Their main differences are in their underlying philosophy and how directly they focus on the process of creating a sacred text. I have had success with all four. You can, of course, always choose to create your own model based on an amalgamation of these and your own ideas.

You can decide on the group type individually and then form a group or reverse the process and make deciding the model your group's first order of business. While sifting through the choices, look for the one that best suits you and your group's creative style, personality, group dynamics, and belief systems. Feel free to tinker with the process as you go to adapt it more closely to your needs.

Story Circles: Story circles are peer-run groups with little formal structure. Their primary focus is to champion and encourage the creative process. They accomplish this by developing a group dynamic that offers a nurturing and safe space for individuals to birth their own story. Group members provide unconditional support, reflect the good and beautiful present in each person's process, and perceive their role in the development of another's story as a sacred gift. Success is seen as inevitable when it is supported by the power of the group's belief in each individual's ability to reach his or her highest potential.

An underlying philosophy that Spirit is the source of our creative abilities gives this model a spiritual orientation. While there is no specific tradition associated with it, an opening or closing prayer that seeks Spirit's presence and guidance is often offered. The discussion of the role of faith and the sacred in our creative process is commonplace.

Organization of story circles is very loose and typically involves no formal leadership or meeting structure. Time is spent allowing all members to share where they are in the process and how they believe the group can help them reach their goal. There are only a few guidelines regarding things such as the number of members or the length of meetings. Cross-talk and advice giving are allowable if members agree they would be helpful. If you are seeking a flexible group design, this might be the best choice for you. Also, because so much of your process involves creation, this group model is well suited for supporting the compilation of your personal sacred text.

For further information on creating a story circle, please refer to Julia Cameron's *The Artist's Way*. The underlying philosophy and concept is similar to what she calls sacred circles. In her appendix she provides basic rules for running this type of group and a prayer she wrote for opening or closing the meeting.

Sacred Circles: This model is also a peer-run group yet with more structure than a story circle. The focus of a sacred circle is to promote personal and spiritual growth. This is accomplished through a process of allowing each member to speak without interruption and be heard by others who are listening without any personal agenda. The process has basic guidelines and a recommended format that create a nurturing and safe space for all participants.

Robin Deen Carnes and Sally Craig have written a beautiful book entitled *Sacred Circles* about this model if you are seeking additional information. They outline all of the details for forming this type of group and also provide personal examples. Although they specifically address this process as relating to women's groups, I have found it to be successful for mixed-gender memberships.

Master Mind Groups: The late Reverend Jack Boland developed the Master Mind Principle and group process while he pastored the nationally renowned Church of Today. The primary purpose of this group model is to attain personal and spiritual growth through the setting of goals, focusing of positive energy, and envisioning of success. Meeting with your Master Mind partners and keeping a Goal Achiever's Journal are equally important parts of the process.

The term "Master Mind" is comparable to what I refer to as Spirit. According to the group's philosophy, focusing the power of positive thought can manifest a powerful connection with Spirit that will result in amazing personal growth and achievement. As you share your hopes, dreams, and struggles with the group, everyone becomes connected to Spirit in a unified vision of seeing you already having achieved the highest and best resolution. When you struggle with doubt, other members can serve as a conduit of the power of positive thinking by believing and holding true for you what you cannot for yourself. While the concept and its power are clearly defined, note that the format of meetings is not too structured.

While this process seems the least suited to creating a personal sacred text, it is easily adaptable. This model is also my favorite. I use bits and pieces of its powerful focusing and envisioning process in almost every group I facilitate. I also have been personally involved in a Master Mind group, and although none of the other group members was creating a personal sacred text, my process was amazingly accelerated through their support and energy. The group has been incredibly powerful in helping me reach my potential in every area of my life. If you are goal oriented and interested in a model that will support various aspects of your personal and spiritual development, this is the perfect process for you.

Master Mind materials are not readily available in bookstores. Your best bet for finding them locally may be a Unity or New Thought church. You also can order the journals and an assortment of related materials from the Church of Today at P.O. Box 280, Warren, Michigan, 48090. They also accept phone orders at 800-256-1984.

Road Warrior Groups: This is the model I have personally developed to support the process of creating a personal sacred text. It is the most structured of those presented because it was designed to work efficiently within a short time frame with a large number of participants. In order to function under those conditions, a tighter format is a necessity. While this model encourages spiritual exploration and personal growth, these are not the focus of the group. It can be difficult to establish the type of intimacy and trust necessary to nourish those two areas with a large group that is meeting only for several weeks or months. Therefore, the primary emphasis is on the process of compiling, writing, and assembling a sacred text.

Road Warrior groups typically meet for two hours once a week over two to three months. They function well with three members or with as many as twenty. Larger groups are accommodated by dividing into small groups of three during the personal-sharing portion of the meeting. A facilitator is appointed for each week and functions as a time-keeper and agenda monitor. Ground rules similar to those I provided earlier are established at the first meeting.

Road Warrior group gatherings begin with a brief check-in allowing each member to share for a specified period of time, usually one or two minutes, about his or her week. This is followed by an opportunity for members to read aloud to the whole group selections they found or wrote during the week that were particularly meaningful to them. I usually limit this to three to five people for the sake of time. Who can read is determined on the basis of a sign-up sheet on a first-come, first-served policy. Next the group divides into trios and spends approximately thirty minutes sharing their experiences in any way they wish. They can talk about what they explored or thought about during the week or they can read from additions they made or are considering making to their text. Following this the entire group reassembles for a brief discussion of any problems people might be having with the process, such as how to document or assemble their text. The meetings conclude with a closing prayer.

Although Road Warrior groups can seem a bit sterile compared to the other models presented, they familiarize people with the concept of creating a personal sacred text in a short period of time. The group setting allows people to take advantage of the collective energy and wisdom that would not be present if they were learning on their own. For this reason a Road Warrior model may be a good way to start your group if most of your members are unfamiliar with creating a personal sacred text. As everyone becomes more comfortable with the process, you can move into one of the less-structured and more growth-oriented styles.

Publication

YOU MAY WISH to share your scripture writing with a broader audience than a partnership or group allows. Its power might be so substantial that you feel others would benefit from it as you have. If these statements are true for you, publication is an option to consider. A variety of venues would be suitable for this purpose:

- Churches and spiritual community newsletters
- Alternative press magazines or specialty newspapers that focus on spirituality and personal growth
- National magazines and newsletters, such as Unity's *Daily Word*, which accept submissions of poetry and prose from

the public. Browse through the periodicals or writer's resource section of your local library to pursue those options

- Poetry and prose contests that publish winning entries

- Opportunities on the World Wide Web; check them carefully though, especially in terms of protecting your copy-
  right

- Self-publishing a book of scripture written by you or the
  members of your group; for guidance, read Tom and
  Marilyn Ross's most recent edition of *The Complete Guide
  to Self-Publishing*

- My website, newsletter, and possible future anthologies of
  scripture writing (see page 258 for more information)

It is important to remember that publishing your scripture writing is a very public way of declaring your beliefs and thoughts. While it
is a great gift to many readers, others may not be so receptive. Take care
to consider the risks and benefits carefully before you pursue this
option.

Leaving Your Legacy

LEAVING YOUR personal sacred text as a legacy for generations to
come is a powerful way of involving community in your process. If
you decide that you do not wish to share your personal sacred text with
anyone in your lifetime, consider leaving it as a legacy for your children
or community. While I have not yet had the opportunity to do so, I can
envision the power of hearing excerpts from someone's text read at a funeral or life celebration. Those in attendance would gain the opportunity to know the wisdom and growth the person had attained in this life
and to learn something from his or her journey. Future generations inside and outside a family can benefit from all the hard work the person
put into assembling a personal sacred text. In my opinion, family photo

albums and diaries pale in comparison to the powerful legacy your work can be to those who follow and will follow you.

THERE ARE SO MANY options to consider when deciding if and how you will share your sacred text with others. Formal and informal methods are available, with each category having another set of choices. Give yourself the time to travel and explore on your own for a while. Then choose a method that is suited to your specific needs. Explore and experiment until you find the best one or two. Don't settle for something that doesn't fit. You deserve to be involved in a supportive relationship that fits you perfectly—after all, that is what the process of creating a personal sacred text is all about.

Bibliography

Ahmed, Ali Jimale, and Ahmed Ali, trans., *Al-Qur'an: A Contemporary Translation* (Princeton Publishing Company, 1988).

Albom, Mitch, *Tuesdays with Morrie: An Old Man, a Young Man, and the Last Great Lesson* (Doubleday, 1997).

Aldrich, Anne Hazard, *Notes From Myself: A Guide to Creative Journal Writing* (Carroll & Graf Publishers, 1998).

Anderson, Sarah, ed., *Heaven's Face Thinly Veiled: A Book of Spiritual Writing by Women* (Shambhala Publications, 1998).

Armstrong, Karen, ed., *Visions of God: Four Medieval Mystics and Their Writings* (Bantam, 1994).

Arnold, E. V., trans., *The Rig Veda* (AMS Press, 1972).

Aschmann, Lisa, *500 Songwriting Ideas for Brave and Passionate People* (Mix Books/Cardinal Books, 1997).

Bach, Richard, *Jonathan Livingston Seagull: A Story* (Avon, 1995).

Baldwin, Christina, *Life's Companion: Journal Writing as a Spiritual Quest* (Bantam, 1990).

Ban Breathnach, Sarah, *Simple Abundance: A Daybook of Comfort and Joy* (Warner Books, 1995).

Bancroft, Anne, ed., *Weavers of Wisdom: Women Mystics of the 20th Century* (Arkana, 1989).

Besserman, Perle, ed., *Teachings of the Jewish Mystics* (Shambhala Publications, 1998).

Bloch, Douglas, ed., *I Am with You Always: A Treasury of Inspirational Quotations, Poems, and Prayers* (Bantam, 1992).

Bloomfield, Harold, *Happiness: The TM Program, Psychiatry, and Enlightenment* (Dawn Press, 1976).

Bluestien Davis, Susan, *After Midnight: The Life and Death of Brad Davis* (Pocket Books, 1997).

Bode, Richard, *First You Have to Row a Little Boat: Reflections on Life and Living* (Warner Books, 1995).

Book of Mormon (The Church of Jesus Christ of Latter-day Saints, 1830).

Brussat, Frederic, and Mary Ann, *Spiritual Literacy: Reading the Sacred in Everyday Life* (Simon & Schuster, 1996).

Burns, Kephra, and Susan L. Taylor, eds. *Confirmation: The Spiritual Wisdom That Has Shaped Our Lives* (Anchor Books, 1997).

Cameron, Julia, *The Artist's Way* (Tarcher/Putnam, 1992).

Camphausen, Rufus C., *The Spirit Library* (Inner Traditions International, 1992).

Carmody, Denise Lardner, and John Tully Carmody, *Mysticism: Holiness East and West* (Oxford University Press, 1996).

Carnes, Robin Deen, and Sally Craig, *Sacred Circles* (HarperSanFrancisco, 1998).

Carrington, Patricia, *Learn to Meditate Kit* (Element Books, 1998).

Casey, Michael, *Sacred Reading: The Ancient Art of Lectio Divina* (Liguori Publications, 1996).

Castelli, Jim, ed., *How I Pray* (Ballantine Books, 1994).

Chambers, Oswald, *My Utmost for His Highest* (Dodd, Mead & Company, 1932).

Chinmoy, Sri, *The Three Branches of India's Life-Tree: Commentaries on The Vedas, The Upanishads, and The Bhagavad Gita* (Aum Publications, 1996).

Citron, Stephen, *Songwriting: A Complete Guide to the Craft* (Limelight Editions, 1990).

Cleary, Thomas, trans., *The Dhammapada* (Bantam, 1994).

Cleary, Thomas, trans., *The Essential Confucius: The Heart of Confucius' Teachings in Authentic I Ching Order* (HarperSanFrancisco, 1992).

Cleary, Thomas, trans., *The Essential Koran: The Heart of Islam* (Castle Books, 1993).

Cleary, Thomas, trans., *Unlocking the Zen Koan* (North Atlantic Books, 1997).

Cloverdale Sumrall, Amber, and Patrice Vecchione, eds., *Storming Heaven's Gate: An Anthology of Spiritual Writings by Women* (Plume, 1997).

Cohen, Alan, *A Deep Breath of Life: Daily Inspiration for Heart-Centered Living* (Hay House, 1996).

Cohen, Alan, *The Dragon Doesn't Live Here Anymore* (Fawcett Books, 1993).

Conze, Edward, trans., *Buddhist Wisdom Books, Containing the Diamond Sutra and the Heart Sutra* (Allen & Unwin, 1958).

Covey, Stephen, *Seven Habits of Highly Effective People* (Fireside, 1989).

Culligan, Kevin, Mary Jo Meadow, and Daniel Chowning, *Purifying the Heart: Buddhist Insight Meditation for Christians* (Crossroad Publishing, 1994).

Daily Word: Love, Inspiration, and Guidance for Everyone (Daybreak Books, 1997).

Dann, Patty, *The Baby Boat* (Hyperion, 1998).

Davich, Victor N., *The Best Guide to Meditation* (Renaissance Books, 1998).

Dawson, Sophie, *The Art and Craft of Papermaking: Step-by-Step Instructions for Creating Distinctive Handmade Paper* (Lark Books, 1997).

Dening, Sarah, *The Everyday I Ching* (St. Martin's, 1997).

DeWaal, Esther, *The Celtic Way of Prayer: The Recovery of the Religious Imagination* (Doubleday, 1997).

Dunn, Phillip, *Prayer: Language of the Soul* (Daybreak Books, 1997).

Edmonds, Margot, and Ella E. Clark, *Voices of the Winds: Native American Legends* (Facts On File, 1989).

Eliot, Alexander, *The Global Myths: Exploring Primitive, Pagan, Sacred, and Scientific Mythologies* (Continuum Publishing Group, 1993).

Elliott, William, *Tying Rocks to Clouds: Meetings & Conversation with Wise and Spiritual People* (Quest Books, 1995).

Emerson, Ralph Waldo, *Nature and Other Writings* (Shambhala Publications, 1994).

Erhlich, Dimitri, *Inside the Music: Conversations with Contemporary Musicians about Spirituality, Creativity, and Consciousness* (Shambhala Publications, 1997).

Falk, Marcia, *The Book of Blessings: A New Prayer Book for the Weekdays, the Sabbath, and the New Moon Festival* (HarperSanFrancisco, 1996).

Fenchuk, Gary W., ed., *Timeless Wisdom* (Cake Eaters, 1994).

Fennimore, Flora, *The Art of the Handmade Book: Designing, Decorating, and Binding One-of-a-Kind Books* (Chicago Review Press, 1992).

Foster, Richard, and James Bryan Smith, eds., *Devotional Classics* (HarperSanFrancisco, 1993).

Fox, John, *Finding What You Didn't Lose: Expressing Your Truth and Creativity Through Poem-Making* (Tarcher/Putnam, 1995).

Friedman, Lenore, and Susan Moon, eds., *Being Bodies: Buddhist Women on the Paradox of Embodiment* (Shambhala Publications, 1997).

Funk, Robert W., Roy W. Hoover, and The Jesus Seminar, *The Five Gospels: The Search for the Authentic Words of Jesus* (Polebridge Press, 1993).

Furlong, Monica, *Visions and Longings: Medieval Women Mystics* (Shambhala Publications, 1996).

Gach, Gary, ed., *What Book? Buddha Poems from Beat to Hiphop* (Parallax Press, 1998).

Gardener, John, and Francesca Gardener, eds., *Quotations of Wit and Wisdom* (W. W. Norton & Company, 1975).

Gawain, Shakti, *Creative Visualization* (Bantam, 1983).

Gellman, Marc, and Thomas Hartman, *How Do You Spell God?: Answers to the Big Questions from Around the World* (Morrow Junior Books, 1995).

Gibran, Kahlil, *The Prophet* (Alfred A. Knopf, 1923).

Gillette, Steve, and Mark Moss, *Songwriting and the Creative Process: Suggestions and Starting Points for Songwriters* (Sing Out! Publications, 1995).

Gire, Ken, *Between Heaven and Earth* (HarperSanFrancisco, 1997).

God's Treasury of Virtues: An Inspirational Collection of Stories, Quotes, Hymns, Scriptures, and Poems (Honor Books, 1995).

Goss, Linda, and Clay Goss, eds., *Jump Up and Say! A Collection of Black Storytelling* (Touchstone, 1995).

Gribetz, Jessica, *Wise Words: Jewish Thoughts and Stories Through the Ages* (William Morrow & Company, 1997).

Hall, Thelma, *Too Deep for Words: Rediscovering Lectio Divina* (Paulist Press, 1994).

Harcourt, Giles, and Melville Harcourt, eds., *Short Prayers for the Long Day* (Triumph Books, 1978).

Hart, William, *The Art of Living: Vipassana Meditation as Taught by S. N. Goenka* (HarperSanFrancisco, 1987).

Herzberg, Abel J. (Jack Santcross, trans.), *Between Two Streams: A Diary of Bergen-Belsen* (St. Martin's, 1997).

His Holiness the Dalai Lama, *The Good Heart: A Buddhist Perspective on the Teachings of Jesus* (Wisdom Publications, 1996).

Hoff, Benjamin, *The Tao of Pooh* (Penguin Books, 1982).

Hollander, John, and Eavan Boland, eds., *Committed to Memory: 100 Best Poems to Memorize* (Riverhead Books, 1997).

Hope, Jane, *The Secret Language of the Soul: A Visual Expression of the Spiritual World* (Chronicle Books, 1997).

Houston, Jean, *A Mythic Life* (HarperCollins, 1996).

Hughes, Dave, *Big Indian Creek: October 23–29, 1994* (Stackpole Books, 1996).

Hughes, Elaine Ferris, *Writing from the Inner Self* (HarperCollins, 1994).

Iglehart Austin, Hallie, *The Heart of the Goddess: Art, Myth, and Meditations of the World's Sacred Feminine* (Wingbow Press, 1991).

Jacobson, Simon, ed., *Toward a Meaningful Life: The Wisdom of the Rebbe Menachem Mendal Schneerson* (William Morrow & Company, 1995).

Jager, Willigis, *Search for the Meaning of Life: Essays and Reflections on the Mystical Experience* (Ligouri Publications, 1995).

James, Cheewa, ed., *Catch the Whisper of the Wind* (Health Communications, 1995).

Johnson, Venice, ed., *Heart Full of Grace: A Thousand Years of Black Wisdom* (Simon & Schuster, 1995).

Kahn, Hazrat Inayat, *The Inner Life* (Shambhala Publications, 1997).

Kamentz, Rodger, *Stalking Elijah: Adventures with Today's Jewish Mystical Masters* (HarperSanFrancisco, 1997).

Keating, Thomas, *Open Mind, Open Heart: The Contemplative Dimension of the Gospel* (Continuum Publishing Group, 1992).

Kenyon, Olga, ed., *800 Years of Women's Letters* (Faber and Faber, 1993).

King, Laurel, *A Whistling Woman Is Up to No Good: Finding Your Wild Woman* (Celestial Arts, 1993).

King, Theresa, ed., *The Spirit Mosaic: Women's Images of the Sacred Other* (Yes International Publications, 1994).

Kingsolver, Barbara, *High Tide in Tucson: Essays from Now or Never* (HarperCollins, 1995).

Kittel, Gerhard, and Gerhard Friedrich, eds. (abridged and translated by Geoffrey W. Bromiley), *Greek Theological Dictionary of the New Testament* (William B. Erdman's Publishing Company, 1985).

Kornfield, Jack, ed., *Teachings of the Buddha* (Shambhala Publications, 1996).

Kurtz, Ernest, and Katherine Ketcham. *The Spirituality of Imperfection: Modern Wisdom from Classic Stories* (Bantam, 1992).

LaPlantz, Shereen, *Cover to Cover* (Sterling Publications, 1998).

Laufer, Joanna, and Kenneth S. Lewis, *Inspired: The Breath of God* (Doubleday, 1998).

Layton, Bentley, *The Gnostic Scriptures* (Doubleday, 1987).

Leeming, David, and Jake Page, *The Mythology of Native North America* (University of Oklahoma Press, 1998).

Lorie, Peter, and Manuela Dunn Mascetti, eds., *The Quotable Spirit: A Treasury of Religious and Spiritual Quotations from Ancient Times to the 20th Century* (Macmillan, 1996).

Mahesh Yogi, Maharishi, *Science of Being and Art of Loving: Transcendental Meditation* (NAL/Dutton, 1994).

Mair, Victor H., trans., *Tao Te Ching: The Classic Book of Integrity and the Way* (Bantam, 1990).

Marks, Kate, *Circle of Song: Songs, Chants, and Dances for Ritual and Celebration* (Full Circle Press, 1995).

Mascaro, Juan, trans., *Bhagavad Gita* (Penguin Books, 1962).

Mascaro, Juan, trans., *Upanishads* (Penguin Books, 1976).

Matthews, John, *The Druid Source Book* (Blanford Press, 1996).

Matthiessen, Peter, *Nine-Headed Dragon River: Zen Journals* (Shambhala Publications, 1998).

McVickar Edwards, Carolyn, ed., *Sun Stories: Tales from Around the World to Illuminate the Days and Nights of Our Lives* (HarperSanFrancisco, 1995).

Mensing, Steve, *Centered: The Handbook of Centering Prayer* (Parabala Books, 1993).

Middlebrook, Christina, *Seeing the Crab: A Memoir of Dying Before I Do* (Doubleday, 1998).

Mieder, Wolfgang, ed., *Illuminating Wit, Inspiring Wisdom: Proverbs from Around the World* (Prentice-Hall, 1998).

Miller, Jay, *Earthmaker: Tribal Stories from North America* (Perigree, 1992).

Mitchell, Stephen, *The Enlightened Heart: An Anthology of Sacred Prose* (Harper Perennial Library, 1993).

Mitchell, Stephen, *The Enlightened Mind: An Anthology of Sacred Prose* (HarperCollins, 1991).

Mitchell, Stephen, *The Essence of Wisdom: Words from the Masters to Illuminate the Spiritual Path* (Broadway Books, 1998).

Moffat, Mary J., and Charlotte Painter, eds., *Revelations: Diaries of Women* (Random House, 1975).

Morrissey, Mary Manin, *Building Your Field of Dreams* (Bantam, 1996).

Moses, Jeffrey, *Oneness: Great Principles Shared by All Religions* (Fawcett-Columbine, 1989).

Muten, Burleigh, ed., *Return of the Great Goddess* (Shambhala Publications, 1994).

Nasar, Sylvia, *A Beautiful Mind: A Biography of John Forbes Nash, Jr.* (Simon & Schuster, 1998).

Nerburn, Kent, and Louise Mengel Koch, *Native American Wisdom* (New World Library, 1991).

Nouwen, Henri J. M., *With Open Hands* (Ave Maria Press, 1972).

Novak, Phillip, *The World's Wisdom: Sacred Texts of the World's Traditions* (HarperSanFrancisco, 1995).

O'Connor, Mike, and Red Pine, eds., *The Clouds Should Know Me by Now* (Publisher's Group West, 1998).

O'Donohue, John, *Anam Cara* (HarperCollins, 1997).

Ollivier, John J., *The Wisdom of African Mythology* (Top of the Mountain Publishing, 1994).

O'Neal, David, ed., *Meister Eckhart, from Whom God Hid Nothing: Sermons, Writings, and Sayings* (Shambhala Publications, 1996).

Orbeck, Kenneth, *Amazing Grace: 366 Inspiring Hymn Stories for Daily Devotions* (Kregel Publications, 1990).

Oster, Eileen F., *The Healing Mind: Your Guide to the Power of Meditation, Prayer, and Reflection* (Prima Publishing, 1996).

Padgett, Ron, ed., *The Teachers and Writers Handbook of Poetic Forms* (Teachers and Writers Collaborative, 1987).

Paul, Susan, *Your Story Matters: Introducing the Pleasures of Personal Writing* (Inner Edge Publishing, 1997).

Pennington, Basil, *The Centering Prayer: Renewing an Ancient Christian Prayer Form* (Doubleday, 1987).

Pennington, Basil, *Lectio Divina* (Crossroads, 1998).

Peterson, Eugene, *The Message* (NavPress, 1993).

Plath, Sylvia (Frances McCullough and Ted Hughes, eds.), *Journals of Sylvia Plath* (Ballantine Books, 1991).

Polman, Bertus Frederick, Marilyn Kay Stulken, Bert Polman, and James R. Sydnor, eds., *Amazing Grace: Hymn Texts for Devotional Use* (Westminster John Knox Press, 1994).

Postema, Don, *Space for God: The Study and Practice of Prayer and Spirituality* (CRC Publications, 1983).

Progoff, Ira, *At a Journal Workshop: Writing to Access the Power of the Unconscious and Evoke Creative Ability* (Jeremy P. Tarcher, 1992).

Rhys-Davids, T. W., and Caroline Rhys-Davids, *Dialogues of the Buddha* (Shambhala Publications, 1977).

Rilke, Rainier Maria (M. D. Herter Norton, trans.), *Letters to a Young Poet* (W. W. Norton & Company, 1994).

Rinpoche, Patrul (Padmakara Translation Group, trans.), *The Words of My Perfect Teacher* (Shambhala Publications, 1998).

Robinson, James M., ed., *The Nag Hammadi Library* (Brill, 1988).

Robinson, Marc, ed., *Altogether Elsewhere: Writers on Exile* (Harvest Books, 1996).

Rosenberg, David, ed., *Communion: Contemporary Writers Reveal the Bible in Their Lives* (Anchor Books, 1996).

Rosenberg, Donna, *Folklore, Myths and Legends: A World Perspective* (NTC Publishing Group, 1996).

Rosenzweig, Rosie, *A Jewish Mother in Shangri-La* (Shambhala Publications, 1998).

Ross, Tom, and Marilyn Ross, *The Complete Guide to Self-Publishing* (Writer's Digest Books, 1994).

Roth, Robert, *Transcendental Meditation* (Donald I. Fine Books, 1994).

Saddington, Marianne, *Making Your Own Paper* (Storey Books, 1992).

Sadleir, Steven S., *The Spiritual Seeker's Guide: The Complete Source for Religions and Spiritual Groups of the World* (Allwon Publishing Company, 1992).

Sarton, May, *Journal of a Solitude* (W. W. Norton & Company, 1992).

Savage, Scott, *The Plain Reader* (Ballantine Books, 1998).

Segal, Suzanne, *Collision with the Infinite: A Life Beyond the Personal Self* (Blue Dove Press, 1996).

Sewell, Marilyn, ed., *Claiming the Spirit Within* (Beacon Press, 1996).

Sewell, Marilyn, ed., *Cries of the Spirit* (Beacon Press, 1991).

Shaughnessey, Edward L., *I Ching: The Classic of Changes* (Ballantine Books, 1996).

Shield, Benjamin, and Richard Carlson, eds., *For the Love of God* (New World Library, 1990).

Simpkins, C. Alexander, and Ann Ellen M. Simpkins, *Principles of Meditation: Eastern Wisdom for the Western Mind* (Charles E. Tuttle & Company, 1996).

Simpkinson, Charles, and Anne Simpkinson, eds., *Sacred Stories: A Celebration of the Power of Stories to Transform and Heal* (HarperSanFrancisco, 1993).

Singh, Rajinder, *Inner and Outer Peace Through Meditation* (SK Publications/Element Books, 1996).

Smith, Garard, ed., *Celebrating Success: Inspiring Personal Letters on the Meaning of Success* (Health Communications, 1997).

Smith, Huston, *The Illustrated World's Religions: A Guide to Our Wisdom Traditions* (HarperSanFrancisco, 1994).

Solomon, Gary, *The Motion Picture Prescription* (Aslan Publishing, 1995).

Steinslatz, Adin, *The Essential Talmud* (Basic Books, 1984).

Steinslatz, Adin, *Talmud, The Steinslatz Edition*, Vol. 10 (Random House, 1994).

Stone, Ira F., *Seeking the Path to Life: Theological Meditations on God and the Nature of People, Love, Life, and Death* (Jewish Lights Publishing, 1992).

St. Ruth, Diana, *Sitting: A Guide to Buddhist Meditation* (Penguin/Arkana, 1998).

Taylor, Susan L., *In the Spirit* (Amistad, 1993).

Terrell, Amber, *Surprised by Grace: A Journey Beyond Personal Enlightenment* (True Light Publishing, 1997).

Thich Nhat Hanh, *Call Me By My True Names: The Collected Poems of Thich Nhat Hanh* (Parallax Press, 1993).

Thich Nhat Hanh, *Fragrant Palm Leaves: Journals 1962–1966* (Parallax Press, 1998).

Thich Nhat Hanh, *Teachings on Love* (Parallax Press, 1997).

Thompson, Marjorie, *Soul Feast: An Invitation to the Christian Spiritual Life* (Westminster John Knox Press, 1995).

Thoreau, Henry David, *Civil Disobedience and Other Essays* (Dover Publications, 1993).

Tom, Michael, ed., *Buddhism in the West: Spiritual Wisdom for the 21st Century* (Hay House, 1998).

Trenoweth, Samantha, *The Future of God: Personal Adventures in Spirituality with Thirteen of Today's Eminent Thinkers* (Millennium Books, 1995).

Tutu, Desmond, ed., *An African Prayer Book* (Doubleday, 1995).

Un, Ko, *Beyond Self: 108 Korean Zen Poems* (Parallax Press, 1997).

Vanessa-Ann, *Making Scrapbooks: A Complete Guide to Preserving Your Treasured Memories* (Sterling Publications, 1998).

Vardey, Lucinda, ed., *God in All Worlds: An Anthology of Contemporary Spiritual Writing* (Pantheon Books, 1995).

Vaughn-Lee, Llewellyn, ed., *Travelling the Path of Love: Sayings of the Sufi Masters* (The Golden Sufi Center, 1995).

Vernes, G., trans., *The Dead Sea Scrolls in English* (Heritage, 1967).

Vilar, Irene, *A Message from God in the Atomic Age* (Pantheon Books, 1996).

Waddell, Helen, trans., *The Desert Fathers* (Vintage Books, 1998).

Waite, A. E., trans., *The Holy Kabbalah* (Citadel Press, 1993).

Washburn, Katharine, John S. Major, and Clifton Fadiman, eds., *World Poetry: An Anthology of Verse from Antiquity to Our Time* (W. W. Norton & Company, 1998).

Wilson, Andrew, ed., *World Scripture: A Comparative Anthology of Sacred Texts* (Paragon, 1995).

Wing, R. L., *The Illustrated I Ching* (Doubleday, 1982).

Young, Serenity, ed., *An Anthology of Sacred Texts by and About Women*, (Crossroads, 1994).

Zaehner, R. C., trans., *Hindu Scriptures* (Alfred A. Knopf, 1992).

Zinsser, William, ed., *Spiritual Quests: The Art and Craft of Religious Writing* (Houghton Mifflin, 1987).

Zipes, Jack, ed., and J. J. Grandville, illus., *Aesop's Fables* (New American Library, 1992).

Author Resources

Workshops and Presentations

The author regularly conducts workshops on how to create a personal sacred text. If you would like a schedule of classes and presentations or are interested in having her speak to your organization, contact her at:

BOBBI L. PARISH, M.A.
RIVER OF TRUTH COUNSELING CENTER
P.O. BOX 2063
GRESHAM, OREGON 97030
503-669-4966
E-MAIL: RIVERTRU@TELEPORT.COM

Newsletter

The author publishes a newsletter, "Notes from the River of Truth," on a quarterly basis. It contains updated resources, hints and suggestions for the creation of your personal sacred text, a workshop and presentation calendar, and scripture-writing selections from readers and workshop participants. If you are interested in a sample copy or subscription information, please contact the author at the above address.

Anthology Submissions

The author is compiling a collection of scripture writing from readers and workshop participants in hopes of publishing an anthology. If you write something, in any genre, that you think others would benefit from reading, please contact the author for submission guidelines.

Web Page

For updated information concerning all of these opportunities, please visit the author's website at: www.riveroftruth.com

Index

About the Author

Bobbi L. Parish is currently a marriage and family therapist. A member of many professional organizations, including the American. Counseling Association, she lives in Gresham, Oregon.